CONVERSATIONS WITH MONSTERS

of related interest

We're All Neurodiverse
How to Build a Neurodiversity-Affirming
Future and Challenge Neuronormativity
Sonny Jane Wise
ISBN 978 1 83997 578 3
eISBN 978 1 83997 579 0

Looking After Your Autistic Self
A Personalised Self-Care Approach to Managing
Your Sensory and Emotional Well-Being
Niamh Garvey
ISBN 978 1 83997 560 8
eISBN 978 1 83997 561 5

So, I'm Autistic
An Introduction to Autism for Young Adults and Late Teens
Sarah O'Brien
ISBN 978 1 83997 226 3
eISBN 978 1 83997 227 0

conversations with

MONSTERS

on mortality, creativity, and
neurodivergent survival

charlotte amelia poe

Illustrated by Tim Stringer

Jessica Kingsley Publishers
London and Philadelphia

First published in Great Britain in 2024 by
Jessica Kingsley Publishers
An imprint of John Murray Press

1

Copyright © Charlotte Amelia Poe 2024
Illustrations copyright © Tim Stringer 2024

A CIP catalogue record for this title is available from the British
Library and the Library of Congress

ISBN 978 1 80501 099 9
eISBN 978 1 80501 100 2

Printed and bound in Great Britain by Clays Ltd

Jessica Kingsley Publishers' policy is to use papers that are natural,
renewable and recyclable products and made from wood grown
in sustainable forests. The logging and manufacturing processes
are expected to conform to the environmental regulations
of the country of origin.

Jessica Kingsley Publishers
Carmelite House
50 Victoria Embankment
London EC4Y 0DZ

www.jkp.com

John Murray Press
Part of Hodder & Stoughton Ltd
An Hachette Company

For Mum and Dad,

Home is wherever you are.

In memory of Amber,

I miss you every day, baby girl,
even after all this time.

Life, although it may only be an accumulation of anguish, is dear to me, and I will defend it.
Mary Shelley, *Frankenstein*

Dear reader,

If this is your copy, take a pen and write your name and the date somewhere in these pages. I won't tell anyone. If this isn't your copy - maybe do it anyway. It's our secret.

Contents

Things I like, December 2022:

lonely blue whales, acoustic guitars, girls who recite poetry, the static on vinyl records, glow in the dark stars, taxidermy, The Amazing Devil (band), shrikes, blood moons, roller skates, longboards, bad tattoos, trickster spirits, necromancers, poiesis, the call of the void, film photography, *Annihilation* (film), bonfires, haunted books, ghosts, hag stones, bleach blonde hair, foxes, London, dried flowers, leather jackets, bisexuality, bards, Taylor Swift (musician), too big hoodies, Tasmanian tigers, boys who paint their nails, calligraphy, fake freckles, real freckles, the colour yellow, unexplained bruises, trees with initials carved into the bark, memorial benches, gravestones covered in ivy, plush axolotls, sunflowers, fairy rings, singing loudly, deep voices, Sweet Gene Vincent (song), making lists, tie dye, art prints, enamel pins, tarot cards, chipped mugs, telling stories, thinking about the end of the world, not writing lists of things I dislike, monsters that aren't really monsters at all, forests dark and deep.

author's note

In 2019, I published my first book, *How To Be Autistic*. It was a memoir, detailing the entirety of my life up until the point I wrote it. It was brutally honest, probably to a fault, and it named people and places that didn't need or want to be named. I was, perhaps, a little naïve when I wrote it, never expecting thousands of people to read it. I felt like I had a duty to write it, to tell my story and to try to do some good in the world. I still feel that duty, though now I understand a little more the nuances of storytelling and what it means to display your life to the public, and how scary that can be.

I have received so many messages from people who have read *How To Be Autistic* who could relate to parts or all of it. People have been diagnosed because of it. It has changed lives. This is such an honour and a privilege, and I am so grateful to have been a part of it.

Conversations with Monsters is not picking up where *How To Be Autistic* left off. Where *How To Be Autistic* was specific in its honesty, I now want to write about the things I left out, intentionally or otherwise, with the added veil of metaphor.

I want you to know that when I call myself a monster, I am only speaking to my own experience. When I call myself a ghost or a haunting, once again it is my own experience. All of this is only me, talking about me, for you, as though we were sitting beside each other at the campfire. It is, best described, one long prose poem, all of it true, but written as a kind of fiction.

In this book I talk about trauma, depression, anxiety, autism, suicidality, the end of the world, and the deaths of family members. All of these subjects are handled with the care I can ascribe to them, but ultimately, I wanted to tell you the truth of them, and that might be hard to read at times. I urge you to take a moment if you need it, or to put the book down if it becomes too much. One of my biggest fears is to harm someone with my words, so I want to warn you in advance. Here be monsters.

I am speaking only for myself, and not my family, or friends, or any community, or any organization. These are my thoughts and my thoughts alone. I do not make myself an ambassador for anything other than the work you're about to read.

Writing is the greatest joy in my life, and I am so grateful that I get to do it time and time again. Thank you for joining me on this journey. I hope you enjoy this adventure. Come, I hear there are thousands of words just waiting for you!

All facts were true at the time of writing. The Doomsday Clock has long since skipped forward since I wrote this, but I want us to remain in the bubble I was in as I put this down into words, even if that means messing with time itself. So, some things aren't true any more. Isn't that strange?

INTRODUCTION

doomsday: one hundred seconds to midnight

I'm a little bit afraid of the world ending. I think there are big ways and small ways for it to do so. I keep coming back to it, you see?

When I was in high school, an English teacher showed us the first half of *When the Wind Blows*. The Doomsday Clock sat at five minutes to midnight, he said, and I stayed awake, muddled and confused, watching the numbers tick over in bed waiting for the world to explode. It didn't. And we were never shown the second half of *When the Wind Blows*. There had been complaints from parents. Too many sleepless nights, too much nuclear annihilation.

The Doomsday Clock currently sits with heavy hands at one hundred seconds to midnight. I don't know what to do with that information. I'm not sure I'm *supposed* to do anything, except worry. There's nothing I can do. I can think about shadows blasted into walls and pavements, I can think about a sudden blinding flash followed by a desperate certainty that this is really and truly it – or.

Or is a very big word for two letters.

I am writing this because you are in the future. It is impossible that you are not. There is no way I can exist with you and write these words at the same time. You exist, now. I exist, now. But we both have different ideas of what now is, do you see?

Perhaps you don't. That's okay. I've always been different, *wrong*, my brain is wired in a way that lends itself to concepts and ideas that follow strange alleyways to things that cause a vast array of spirals. Neurodivergence, in my case a rather stunning display of autism, is a gift that will leave you lost in a forest with some very strange footprints to follow.

And yeah, you'll want to go home a lot of the time. God, if that isn't my life's great motto – I want to go home. But the older I get, the more I realize there is no such place as home, not really. I think maybe I had it as a child, but now there is nowhere that is wholly safe and wholly mine and wholly unhaunted.

I'm going to tell you some ghost stories. Yes, there's a campfire in this forest, and we're all going to gather around in our different temporalities and toast vegan marshmallows and shiver our spines as we wonder about mortality and what it means to even exist at all. How we're all ghosts, and how we all haunt places and people, all the time. This book is haunted. It is our honour as creatures caught within this universe to do this haunting, and to leave little reminders of ourselves along the way. We are graffiti on walls and chalk on pavements and sandcastles on the beach. All potentially temporary, but god, aren't we beautiful whilst we last?

We all want to be remembered, I think. I think that's the most human thing there is to want. No matter how strong or loud the call of the void may be, we at least want someone to know we heard it. We want to be loved, to have loved, to have mattered. We perhaps want to change the world – in a way that is big or small. And we do. It's impossible not to. We all change the world all the time, in ways we might not even realize.

I remember sitting in the car waiting for my dad to pick something up. A stranger walked past. I couldn't tell you what she looked like now, but I remember she was beautiful, confident, and unapologetically gay. And god, I loved her in that minute and I carry that feeling with me still. She doesn't know I exist, she never ever will, but I remember her as a few seconds of a kind of purity and awe that reminded my heart how to pump and my brain how to spark.

How many people, do you think, have looked at you and felt that kind of awe? Don't say none. It's not true. You have no idea how awe-inspiring you are. I know this because I know people – brilliant, brilliant people, who don't realize that they are woven with magic. And I tell them, over and over, because I hope one day they'll believe me.

All of this, I want to call this a kind of letter to you, almost like a telegram or something, winging its way to you through time and space and being translated from my brain to yours - this letter, it's the opposite of the void calling. You know, when you stand near a railing and realize it'd be the work of an instant to climb over and feel what it'd be like to fly, or those lonely nights when your thoughts go dark and oppressive and you want to claw at your skin until you don't hate yourself any more - all of this, I am giving to you as a hand on your shoulder, urging you back to safer ground.

I find myself, again and again, on the edge of all things, wondering when it'll get better. I had been promised a life, and yet it seems I get mere snatches of the damn thing. My brain is a fantastic liar, you see. Perhaps yours is too. It'll never tell you the truth of things. Things are bad, often. But sometimes things are so good. I can never see the good when there is so much bad, and this past year has been a deluge of bad, but I am promising you some good. Because I think I need to promise that to myself, too.

When the sky is dark and the night is cold and your skin goosebumps and you feel more alone than

you've ever felt, this is when I want to haunt you.
In your past, my present, our future, you know? It's
crazy, right? An attempt at comfort written across
the timeline. I'm going to tell you some stories and
they're all going to be true in different ways. I have a
pocket knife and I am etching my initials in the tree
bark, knowing that they will grow upwards and away
from me. I want you to put yours there too.

Life is really fucking hard and it always feels like
the end of the world. If you watch the news, they'll
probably tell you it is. See, I don't know. Obviously
there's the chance of some cosmic irony preventing
you from ever reading this, but perhaps you are.
Which means the world hasn't ended yet. Which
means it might keep not ending.

Does that make sense?

Here's a thing.

When I was a child, I was at the beach with my
dad and there was a snowstorm, sudden and all-
encompassing. I couldn't see anything but white,
the world was a flurry around me and I couldn't

do anything. It was scary and beautiful and I was lost whilst being in the same place I had been five minutes before. My dad guided me out. We got home safely. My mum made me hot chocolate, and I remember she made it in the microwave, and I remember it was the first time I'd had hot chocolate.

Here's another thing.

I was scared a lot as a child. I learned how to be scared. I hate that I learned how to anticipate fear, that it's been drilled into my bones until it's beyond muscle memory, it's second nature. A lot of things are really scary. This world – I don't know if I'm built for it. It doesn't take kindly to brains that don't work how they're supposed to. Though, I would argue, there is not a single brain on this planet equipped to cope with the world as we know it now.

Here's the third thing.

I'm telling you about the snowstorm and I'm telling you about fear because none of this is linear. Healing isn't linear. The dams burst open all the time. Old scars and new. Fear springs eternal. My brain was *wrong wrong wrong* and therefore I was *wrong wrong wrong*.

I refuse to accept that, though. I refuse to pass on the damage done to me as some kind of perpetuity of trauma. This exists because I need to remember that I got out of the snowstorm and that I got to be warm again. And yes, after that came the bad years. But I have to believe that the snowstorms continue to pass and the microwave will continue to ding and there will be a mug of hot chocolate waiting again. Can you believe that with me, for however long this journey takes?

Can I take your hand, and lead you through the forest? I have some things I want to show you, some things I want to talk about. I'm still trying to make sense of it all myself. This is a ghost story in present tense. I need to do this. The most human thing, right?

What time is it where you are? Are you happy? Are you warm? How many seconds to midnight?

Do you know how brilliant you are? How utterly

unprecedented you are? Has anyone told you lately? I'm telling you now. The whole universe, all of it, and you're the only you that exists. That must be some kind of magic.

Let's go on an adventure.

i want to tell you that i am extraordinary and not be a liar

I am trying to think of a way to introduce myself that doesn't seem overt and impractical. I have told you about the end of the world, and now I'm expected to fill in all the gaps between that and me, and boy, there are a lot of gaps. I wrote my life out in short little chapters and I called it *How To Be Autistic*, and I never read it again, because I had peeled my skin and shown you the delicate organs inside, and that was scary. Sometimes, late at night, I like to think about how many copies of that book I have sold, and then I can really freak myself out.

I want to shroud myself with a degree of metaphor from here on out. You can go and poke around at the vivisection of my life if you want, or you can follow me into the forest with my face half covered with a mask and I will tell you only what you need to know. In return, I will ask nothing of you that you do not want to give. Is that fair?

I am autistic. I was diagnosed when I was twenty-one, when the trauma had settled in and made a home at the back of my throat. I'd like to say that things are better now, that I got help and that I know what I'm supposed to be doing, but that's not true. You know things don't work that way. The tide ebbs and flows, always returning to the shore as readily as it shies away from it, and so I bob along, trying to keep my head above water and to catch my breath where I can.

I have tried the performance of gender and found myself lacking. There is nowhere in the binary that feels like a box I want to tick, and so I choose not to. This has followed me through life since before I had a name for it, and despite the dysphoria, god, the dysphoria, I wouldn't change it. I like being a strange third thing, even as the political climate turns rancid and I become afraid of where this will all lead. I cannot, *will* not, pretend to be something I'm not for an easy life.

I feel, perhaps, that that is something of a thesis statement.

I think a lot about monsters, about how they are shaped, how they growl with sharp tooth and claw, and how they are feared rather than afraid. It is difficult to love a monster, and as I look in the mirror, my faceblindness offering me newness at every glance, I see a certain kind of monster, and I wonder who first applied the label, and when it started to fit so well. Was it the children who yelled slurs across the playground, was it the adults who misconstrued and misunderstood until I started to twist and change and my eyes flashed and became slightly more inhuman? Does the inhumane make the inhuman? Did my trauma make me into something new, and if so, does that make me evil, or does it make me a survivor? Are all monsters just trying to survive, in their way, running from the silver bullets that poison and burn just as readily as words and the passive inaction that frustrates and can never be reasonably explained?

Why didn't you do anything, why didn't you do more, why did my life become a sideshow, a horror show, a performance for the crowd? Let me make sense of it, let me understand why you did this. What you did and didn't do.

There are so many people I would haunt in the middle of the night if I only could, though I am not as kind as the ghosts in *A Christmas Carol*; I fear I seek retribution and I am more propelled by anger than I am by any kind of closure. I don't know if I want them to learn from their mistakes. I want them to pay.

Monsters are not kind, so maybe I am a monster.

Maybe as well as the monsters all around me, I am a monster too.

There is freedom in accepting the monstrous and finding the sharpness of your bite and the way you can wield it. You can shape your words around your teeth and use them with a care that others lack. You can use those claws to carve pictures that are beautiful despite and because of what you've been through. You can claim the fearlessness of the wolf, the way it can skulk in the shadows, but remember that it also learned to be treated as something beloved by man. What a fantastic trick to play. There are footprints, preserved, of a child and a wolf walking side by side to collect water. A parent trusted this companion with their child's life, barely domesticated, and was repaid for that kindness with kindness in return.

I accept the things that make others afraid of me, and I wrap them around myself like a cloak, obscuring and hiding the ways they can actually hurt me. I cover myself in tattoos - an art form so old that cultures are named for it, and I see the way I am treated for the ink under my skin and I understand why people once used them for protection.

I am cosmically very small, no gaping maw or supernova here, but really, I am human and that is all I know how to be. Whether you see me as something that is other is not my fault and there is little I can do to change your mind. It is easier, maybe, to be misunderstood than to find the words, over and over again, to explain the very existence that is me.

I feel, and have felt, that I have to be extraordinary. And not in the way that we are all extraordinary by virtue of our birth, of our lives sparking bright and tracing gold across maps and time. No, I need to tell you this. Ever since I was a child, I knew I had to be shockingly extraordinary. Which, as someone who struggles in mediocrity, was a blow.

I have thrown myself at ridiculous things that were designed by a world more neurotypical than I can relate to. Television, radio, books, writing, maintaining a presence online despite the fear that someone, anyone, could say anything, and oh, those silver bullets, you know?

I want to make my parents proud. I am so deeply afraid of failing. It is the ongoing mission statement, more so than any other; if *I want to go home* is the mantra, then my parents' pride is the motivation to stay outside.

I am told that I have not failed in this task. I cannot

bring myself to believe this. I have to be more, always, in impossible ways, I have to shape myself anew and to sparkle brighter and to bite back the rejections that threaten to spill from my lips and to not let it hurt me when people say I am not good enough. Oh! The rejections. God, the rejections. So many, all the time, because what I want to do is not rare or special. People are doing it better than me every day, you see?

I don't want to be the best, but I don't want to be average either. I want to flame bright for as long as I can, fire biting at the wood and churning it up and allowing it to make me bigger and stronger in the fireplace that is all of this. I want to keep people warm, the same way my mum did when she gave me that hot chocolate all those years ago. I want to be the bonfire people who settle around to tell stories of kinder lives, lives well lived, guided half by fate and half by chance, these golden lives with the best possible outcomes.

I have been shaped, as readily as clay, into what I am now, this needy desperate creature that shuns touch but craves it all at once. I have been hurt and

I have hurt, and I need to find a middle ground, a no man's land that breeds neutrality and allows for the healing of wounds, if only for a little while. I have been so lost, so so lost. Time and friendship have been stripped from me and I find myself turning in the wind and wondering where they went to.

Call me an optimist, a damned optimist, but it all comes back. It never looks the same way when it does, but I promise you, it all comes back. You find friends with new faces, and time gives you a chance to breathe and suddenly you can run with it, and whether that's on four legs or two, it doesn't matter - whether you are monster or man, as long as you can keep up and you can find a way to love the form you take, that is what matters. Do no harm, but do not allow harm to be done to yourself either.

If I had been born different, with a different quirk in my brain, then none of who I am would exist. At a very base level, I would be shaped differently, my thoughts would run in directions that are utterly alien to me. And do I envy the existence I never had? Of course I do. Maybe it was simpler. It probably was. Was there either a fork in the road, did I ever go east

when I should have gone west, or was this always
where I was supposed to end up, was there only one
path all along?

I do not recognize who I could have been. I do not
know if I would have liked them. Would they be able
to love my sister's children in the same way that
I do? Would they feel that same protectiveness?
Would they feel the constant drive to create, to leave
this world having made a mark, to have written
across an entire beach a list of demands for a life
I want to create? Would they want everything, all
at once, in a way that is both overwhelming and
impossible?

Would they be afraid?

I will envy them a lack of fear. Always.

But I will not envy them the lack of the monster.
A sharp tongue and sharper teeth and instincts
honed to perfection - I hate how I ended up here
sometimes. But the forest is deeper than we know,
and for every shaded patch of trees, there are
sections where we look up and the sunlight filters

through, and the wolf feels the warmth on its fur and remembers that it is, first of all, a mammal on this earth, and that it has no duty beyond existence, and what it makes of that existence relies on nobody's bidding but its own.

Let's sit in that sunlight now for a while before we continue. Let it warm our skin. The journey will continue. But let us let our monsters rest for a while first.

12th january 2022, and the sudden realization of mortality

Until this year, I had understood mortality through the lens of the death of my cat, Amber. She died eight years ago and I still remember how it felt to hold her, the exact weight of her in my arms, the way she was the most brilliant cat I have ever known, how she loved me more than she loved anybody else, and how I think about her every single day, even now.

The dead cannot speak for themselves, so I will speak perhaps more kindly than they deserve. I have found when putting words down on paper, you must err on the side of kindness with what you immortalize. Be kinder than you need to be, perhaps. So I shall. It is not my job to judge or to eulogize. I am merely discussing the ever-turning wheel that transforms life into ashes.

My grandmother, and I am calling her my grandmother as a kindness, you understand, died on my birthday. It was both expected and not, the way it can be sometimes. It was slow, and then at the end it was quick, though with a lingering that tasted bitter to discuss and that felt deeply savage and wrong.

My grandfather, and yes, he gets that same kindness, followed a few short months later, with less lingering and with somehow more finality than she had provided. The cogs of the wheel turned, and the next generation stepped up to the plate and I felt a kind of fear I have never felt before in my life.

I do not, as a conscious, thinking being, understand death. My brain refuses to comprehend a future where I am not a conscious, thinking being. I am secular in all manners, and yet I believe in a kind of unnameable immortality that I cannot explain. Time, perhaps, offers the answer, in as much as it must loop and overlap, and so we are always alive and always dead, all at once, and therefore we never truly die.

That we die when the last person says our name, when the last person holds us in their hearts, I wonder how true that is. If you are holding this book in fifty years, one hundred, am I still alive to you? Can you imagine what my voice would have sounded like reading these words to you?

The harsh blow of mortality, not even of my own but of my family - I screw myself up against it and shudder away to a corner to hide. I do not want to imagine a world with missing pieces. I don't know how to cope with that. I know that my brain desires sameness, and has an inability to accept change, but there is a level of change I don't think any human being can accept and want to happen.

I am desperately afraid.

If I miss my cat every day, to the point of tears at times, how do I cope when it is more than 'just' a cat?

I don't think I do - is the answer. I don't know, maybe

you can answer for me. Maybe you have experienced this great loss, the ultimate war of being. Maybe you can tell me. I am afraid, reader, so desperately afraid, and this is a kind of fear I am not used to, a kind of fear I cannot anticipate because living in its skin for too long makes me want to vibrate and explode.

It feels like even to talk about it is to usher it into being.

I have never been truly afraid of my own death – perhaps because I didn't believe in it, and perhaps because at many points in my life I would have welcomed it. The oh so common belief in there being some kind of relief to be found in it, the breathing in and out of compressed lungs, getting that good gulp of air after a lifetime of holding your breath – that's what it always felt like to me. It's not true, is it, though? That's what they all tell you. There's no relief, instead there is nothingness. A lack of anything. Something so beyond comprehension that people have to tell themselves stories that go beyond the end of their own world just to cope with it.

This is a letter to you about ends of worlds, and this is an end of a world. Everyone has this end of a world built into them, and it is scarier even than the bombs falling, because it is both more abstract and more concrete all at once.

We cannot envisage it, and yet our mind wanders there nonetheless.

When the monster that is depression weaves its tendrils around my brain and squeezes, I find comfort in the potentiality of that nothingness. I want to stop. Just to stop. I am finished and that is all I want to be. I do not want to be more than a full stop at the end of a sentence. The end. No big finale, no crowd cheering. Just an end.

And yet, here I stand. Somehow startlingly alive despite the worst days, as though I lack the courage of my convictions and as though life has its fish hooks deeper in my skin than I ever realized.

Being alive, the hardest thing any of us will ever do, is addictive. We want more of it, ever more. We don't

want the full stop, the blankness, we just want a
rest point. To press Save Game and not worry about
consequences for a little while. To breathe. The
antithesis of stopping – god, we just want to catch
our breath.

Sometimes, when everything is terrible and my
throat chokes up and my vision smears and my
brain yells at me that everything is pointless, I curl
up and I wish for it all to stop. But – it is not stopping
that I want. Not really. It is change. To be something,
someone else. Someone who is experiencing
different things, who is thinking different thoughts,
who is able to catch their breath and who is able to
cope with whatever has been thrown my way.

I pick up the baseball bat and I sling it up and over
my shoulder, resting my hand against the wood of
it, bracing it against the back of my neck. I am ready
to fight the monsters, because I am fighting for my
life. The most precious, impossible thing. I drum my
fingers in little taps that thud gentle percussions
against my ear drums and I think, yes, the blackness
wants me, but I do not want the blackness. I want
that chink of light that creeps through the curtains

and forces me to screw up my face and try to bury
myself again. I want the daylight! The sun on
my face!

I want all of it!

I want to bite at it!

If we must be alive, we can be so so viciously, so
violently, so beautifully. Not because we owe it to
some ancestor or the great lineage of humanity, but
because we owe it to ourselves. We are here for a
number of years that is so tiny in the grand scheme
of things, this Holocene era stretches far beyond
who we can ever be. Our worlds will end. What the
fuck. Who gave them the right?

So, I suppose, we must enter the battle with the
weapons we forge and we must hit hard and bite
until our jaws ache, and when the darkness tries to
bottle us, we must shine a light in any way we can,
whether it is glow stars on the ceiling or a single
match flickering in a dank cave somewhere, barely
there, but barely there is still *there*, still breathing.
Still thrumming and magnificent and not dead yet.

I can say *I don't want this* through gritted teeth, but it's a lie. I want to be alive so desperately, so much, fish hooks and all tying me to this and the darkness can try to pull me away but god, no, don't you see, the darkness is full of stars and the stars remind me that the sun will rise again and it cannot take me, not yet.

How, then, do I deal with the fact that it might steal someone else? That for all I can rage against the dying of the light, I cannot do it for somebody else?

There is no way to make it rational. There is no comfort to be found in it. I am scared of last words, of the last thing I might say to somebody. I hope that they know that they were so loved. I imagine what I would say in front of a mound of dirt, and I try to turn that inwards and transform it into something I can say now. I am selfish with my own fish hooks, in that I dig in and hold onto people, that I love them without an end.

I do not know how to do this on my own.

I do not wish to learn.

What horrible knowledge that would be.

I try, so hard, to lighten the burden. I am not good at this. Something between me and the world is incompatible with the easing of things. My words trip over each other clumsily and I never quite know what to say. You cannot scream *I love you I love you I love you* into a room full of people, even if that is what you want to do. You have to be more subtle than that, to sidle into every hug and to cherish the way their body wraps around yours and makes your two souls brush against one another.

You must tell people *this reminded me of you and therefore it has love in it*. You must offer kind words and gifts and time and patience. You must push aside the ticking of the clock despite how loud it gets in your ears. Drown it out with the music of laughter and the stupid jokes your father makes. God, it's scary to write that as though it will not be a constant. It churns my stomach and makes my heart burn.

Christmas is coming up, in the timeline I am in. Maybe for you it is summer, but for me it is

December and the air is cold and nips at my skin and the fire roars and the tree is decorated if wonky. My room is a mess of boxes filled with gifts. I have already sent off gifts to my friends around the world and they are in return fighting with shipping and customs to get gifts back to me. There is much talk on the internet of love languages, and gift giving is mine, most certainly. This reminded me of you and therefore it has love in it. All the things I cannot say in words, I can say with an object, no matter how daft. Sometimes people don't understand, because they have a different love language, but when I give a gift it is because I have found something that stores that same love that I feel and I want them to have it forever. To know that I thought of them on some idle Thursday whilst scrolling through the internet and that they brightened my day. Through sheer virtue of their existence. They are out there, out of sight but never out of mind. We are so lucky that we can hold these people close to us even if we cannot see them.

That's what it all is, in the end, isn't it? Filling yourself up with all the stories your friends want to tell you, all the good and bad of your family, the way your nephew sounds like an elf and swears like a sailor, the way you could lose it all in a second but you choose to believe that you never will.

None of these are answers, but I don't think they're questions either. I think they're just how it has to be. We have to be so brave. And with that courage, we have to push back the way we want to scream at the unfairness of it all and to just exist as though tomorrow is a distant country far, far away from us. To tempt fate by loving people.

I don't know.

The cogs of the wheel keep turning.

We all shuffle up a step closer to the grist of the mill.

But god, the sun is shining and it feels good on our skin, and everyone is laughing. So we might as well be here, now.

INTERLUDE
at the bottom of the stairs

my grandparents sit in cardboard boxes
at the bottom of the stairs
nobody is quite sure
what to do with them
so there they remain –
remains,
presumably at some stage they will
be scattered
i don't know, right now we live
with this kind of haunting
this in between of not knowing
and i heard that ashes don't look
like they do on television
but i don't want to check
there is a clock ticking somewhere
and i swear it's coming from my ribcage

i wonder if i'm allowed to feel anything at all
because i didn't really know them
(nor did i really like them)
grief is a tide, nothing so simple
as a lightning strike
it rolls up and over, in and out with the moon
and just as pale, it is a ghost
and just as readily, it is a reminder
all things end
and you too
will find yourself
at the bottom of the stairs.

3
lycanthropy

Monsters again, naturally.

I was live on the radio when I was asked if I would cure my autism if given the opportunity. I stumbled through an answer stating the impossibilities of the question, not willing to go into the eugenics implicit within such a query. The casual dismissal of an entire minority - it's a very strange and uncomfortable idea.

I suppose, in that case, the monster in the room is autism itself. I suppose it is for a lot of people. I am going to be blunt with you, being autistic makes a lot of things really fucking hard. It's a disability, after all.

Autism is the way I think, the way I behave, the way I was born and the way I'll die. It is in every sentence I write, and every word I speak. Sometimes it is a stereotype, sometimes it is not. Sometimes it is good, sometimes it is bad. I do not know who I am without it, because that is an impossible thing to imagine. Some disabilities happen later in life, so there is a before and after. I don't have that comparison to make. All I have is me.

Some things could definitely be easier. Take away the anxiety? I wouldn't even give it a second thought, yes, please, take away the anxiety. The awkward social fumbles? Yes, you could probably get rid of those as well. The way my brain can't seem to understand maths? Well, it would be useful to be able to understand maths, so, yes.

But god, taking away all of me? The entirety of how I think and feel? Stripping me of it all and putting a new human in my place? I don't know how I feel about that.

I know there are a lot of strong opinions, most of them neurotypical. Because the world wasn't built for neurodivergent people, we struggle more, and that is seen as a tragedy, and rather than adapting the world to include us, it seems a simpler answer is to try to cure us. Or to find a way to stop autistic children being born in the first place.

I watch all of this from the side lines, not knowing what to say. Do I wish my life were easier? Yes. But I have to consider all that I'd lose - all the interests and hobbies and the way I can focus on something single-mindedly until it is done - I don't know.

I don't see autism as the monster. I see the abuse doled out to autistic people in the form of electric shocks and conversion therapy as more monstrous than anything we could ever do. I see autistic people rotting away in inpatient hospitals with no care given, I see autistic people undiagnosed and struggling with the system, I see autistic people *diagnosed* and struggling with the system. If we are successful, we are liars. If we are not successful, we are the tragedy writ large.

Do you see now why I have to be extraordinary? People will not accept a mediocre autistic person.

We have to be stunning examples of inspiration if we want to be noticed, we must triumph over adversity and go on to provide motivational speeches and to change the world but only in a way deemed acceptable by neurotypical people who judge us at every step of the way.

These self-appointed experts will write textbooks and go on television and tell newspapers about their findings without consulting a single autistic person. They will ask for our DNA so that they can search for the cause of autism, to narrow it down, and you know that if they somehow find it, there will be fewer autistic children in the world as a result of it. Is that what they want? I think perhaps it is. We are seen as a burden. There are many countries I can never move to because I am autistic and I would require a level of healthcare they are not willing to provide.

I wonder if they think about the damage their actions cause. How we are perpetually second-class citizens held to impossible standards if we want to achieve. What are we supposed to do with that? Surely we internalize it until it turns rancid inside of us and we start to believe it. I have to be extraordinary, right? I don't have a choice. This, right here, has to be extraordinary to be noticed. I have no option but to be impossible.

And then I am seen as inspirational because I survived the system that was designed to break me. That's fucked up, right? Like, objectively, that's fucked up. The system did break me. It broke me so many times. I have mentioned the trauma. It is real and it is never going to go away. That's inspirational, right? All that trauma. That's a real inspiration. Heart-warming, truly.

And yet, here I am. Here I am. I did survive the system. Not everybody does. Not everybody has the support system I did. Not everybody has a mum who will fight to the bitter end for her child. I am one of the lucky ones.

God, that tastes bitter on my tongue.

I want you to consider if you feel lucky. What would you say if they offered you 'the cure'? If they offered to change your very soul to become someone new, someone who wasn't disabled but also wasn't you any more? What would you do?

More importantly, perhaps, what would you feel obligated to do? To be less of a burden, to be a productive member of society, to fit in, to not cause a fuss, to be *normal*?

If there is a spectrum imposed by neurotypical people, it is closer to **TOO AUTISTIC** and **NOT AUTISTIC ENOUGH**. It's hardly a spectrum at all, much closer to a binary. It's funny that we're the ones who are supposed to have black and white thinking, and yet we exist in the shades of grey that neurotypicals do not allow us to operate in.

There is so much to say on this, and at the same time, it is exhausting to consider. It's all so entirely hypothetical anyway, and money being spent on this 'cure' could be spent on enriching the lives of autistic people now. The fact that it's not feels kind of criminal to me, like it shouldn't be allowed. It's just interesting that the biggest charities are the first to blame us for our own abuse, for our own neglect by the system. As though they were powerless to prevent it. It's scary when the so-called guardians are the ones you have to fight against, when they have all the power to spread as much misinformation as they choose to.

It's really hard to exist in a world that is actively hostile to you just because you are you.

It is enough to make you feel hunted.

I have no answers, except that we need more autistic voices, always. If anything I've written so far has motivated you to tell your own story, I urge you to do so. You don't have to write about monsters or ghosts, or anything like I've done. Just be you, unapologetically so, and tell the story they don't want you to tell. You can be vengeance wrapped up in everything they don't want to hear. You can tell other autistic people that it's okay to be autistic, that there is nothing wrong with them. Just like I'm telling you now. It is okay to be autistic. There is nothing wrong with you. It is hard because the system, society, all of it, they make it hard. But it doesn't have to be. We can be loud, right? We can be a beautiful menace. We can cause quite the ruckus, if we try. So maybe we should. They can't ignore us if we all shout at once.

i want to be loved, but not at the cost of my soul

With all that being said, my friend, I am scared of being known.

That's not true. Well.

I am scared of being known in a way that is false.

We overlay our perceptions of people and we count it as objective. People, often neurotypical people, who think they know better, will talk about theory of mind and the 'fact' that autistic people do not understand that other people are thinking, feeling beings. This is not true; I think we can all agree that, yes, sometimes the solipsism does hit hard, but we are aware that we are surrounded by people, people who think and feel just like us, whether it's on the street or in messages on our phones. It is so deeply frustrating to be told something about yourself that is untrue, and for it to be parroted over and over by thousands of people who do not wish to engage with someone whose mind they're actually talking about.

When I dissociate, when reality becomes very strange and a little unreasonable, then I doubt the existence of everything but myself. I understand Descartes when he said *I think therefore I am*, but I lack the ability to acknowledge even my hands as my own. I am in the snowstorm again and the only real things I have are the thoughts in my head, and they are muddled and scared as I stare in the mirror and try to reconcile that what I see is me, the body that houses me, and that if I step outside of the bathroom (why does dissociation always happen in the bathroom? Is it because it is the most private of rooms, where we are ourselves in a way we hope nobody else will ever see us? I don't know) I will see the bodies that house other people and interaction feels stilted and strange, as though everything is a play and I am under-rehearsed and stuttering my lines.

But even through all of the unreality I never doubt the existence of others in a way that devalues their humanity. I remember once, curled over a toilet and feeling like the least real person in the whole of London, overhearing my sister say that it scared her that I didn't think she was real. I wonder if she remembers that, or if it's a memory that I alone hold. She was so young, and I scared her. I hate that.

The dissociation between who I am and who people perceive me to be is awful on a different level to that, though. I know we all feel misunderstood. We rally against it, perhaps. Something within the validation of being known, of people loving you despite knowing you, the blood and guts of it all, that they still love you despite you showing the worst parts of yourself, is so vital. Or maybe you don't feel that, maybe your validation comes from within, and you are raising an eyebrow at the fact that I need to write this down, that I need to scream this at you in black and white and try to make you understand the person that I am trying to be.

I misunderstand myself just as readily as everyone else does, it seems.

When Bruce Springsteen said *I want to change my clothes, my hair, my face*, I feel like he understood what it meant to be human in a way that hasn't been summed up more succinctly before or since. I want to change everything about myself, all the time, and yet I want to be utterly knowable.

A journalist once called it *the mortifying ordeal of being known*.

They described how heartbreaking it is, and how wonderful, all at once.

It's scary, I think, to have someone cradle your beating heart in their hands and to know that they could push their thumbs in and rip it to shreds. I imagine surgeons and gowns and the smell of antiseptic in the air, as a machine keeps me alive and I am cradled by someone I trust to do no harm.

Look at me, I beg of them. Look at me and tell me I am not lacking in your eyes.

In many ways, I find validation in writing. I have always written, I have spilled more secrets than perhaps I should have. I am doing it now. I cannot stop. I can dress up my trauma in a way that is palatable and I can present it to an audience and they can tell me that it is beautiful.

That it helped, in some way.

And yet I feel unseen. Unknown. By my friends, my family, by strangers on the internet. By you. By myself. I am trying to solve the riddle of myself so that I can give the cipher to others. I am shifted two letters to the left and I haven't figured it out yet. There is no Rosetta Stone for what I am trying to be. I don't know who I'm trying to be yet. Why am I trying to be anything, when I could simply be myself?

I do not like myself very much. Seven words, seven deeply angry words that are a lifetime in the making. Maybe you know them too. Maybe you have thought them about yourself. I hope not, but if you have, know that you are not alone in doing so.

If we liked ourselves, nobody would have anything to sell us. So much of the industry we know would

fall apart if we simply acknowledged ourselves
in a way that accepted the flaws and the defects
and if we stopped calling them flaws and defects.
My hair, the wrong colour. My skin, too devoid of
ink. My nose, too crooked and too large by far. My
eyes, well, they simply couldn't see clearly enough,
so I reshaped them in a way that allowed me to
see the leaves on trees and the blades of grass
without glasses on that oh so crooked nose. I am
changeable, so changeable, I will change the parts,
like swapping out components, trying to find the
pieces that fit. I want to be someone worthy of
love, and if I cannot find that love to give to myself,
then as the saying goes, who else could possibly
love me?

I don't believe that, though. I think people can love
you even when you are full of the biggest baddest
hatred for yourself. How dare someone say you
cannot be loved when you are at your lowest? What
a horrific thing to say to somebody. To tell them that
their self-loathing disqualifies them from being
cared for. I have always struggled to find the logic in
this. You cannot force somebody to love who they
are. You can only love them anyway, and support

them when they wish to clear out the weeds and plant the garden anew.

I can say it's not helpful to hate yourself, but people don't always do what is helpful for themselves. I can't simply stop doing it. You can tell me you love me until you're blue in the face, but I will still ask, is this enough? Is it? Is it enough yet? Tell me that I'm good because I cannot judge it for myself.

But the very real question: What if I am not good? What if I am right about all of this?

What objective rating system is there for whether I am a good person or not? The amount of people that tell me I am? That doesn't sound right. Celebrities have millions of fans who are just begging to tell them how loved they are. But I bet the doubt still creeps in. Surely, it must. Is there anybody who believes that they are, if not perfect, then at least fine?

Again, perhaps you are not following me. The great misunderstanding continues! Here, I offer you this peek into the whirring of my brain, and you say, no,

I do not understand, I like myself actually and do not understand why you do not. It's not a decision I made, it's not a decision I continue to make, I think. I don't think you can will yourself into liking yourself, can you? Sure, there are so many affirmation exercises, where you stand in front of a mirror and say nice things to yourself, and maybe they work, and if they do, then that's great, but part of all this mess is that I don't want to look myself in the eye, and I definitely don't want to tell myself untruths.

It's not pretty, is it? This baring of the soul and the pointing out of all the bits that I wish were different. I am so so lucky, in countless ways. Not born in a warzone, not born in famine, not born dying any more than anyone else is. And yet that does not feel like enough. Because I am spoilt by life and all of its many graces. I am spoilt by time and the fact that I have time to sit here and tell you all of this, this navel gazing pondering that helps nobody.

Unless you are finding comfort in being less alone.

I told you I have brilliant, brilliant friends who do

not realize that they are brilliant. I wonder how they feel, if they would tell you the same thing I just told you. Whether or not they can find it within themselves to love the words they write or the art they make. Whether, even outside of productivity, they love the person they are. Whether they *can* love the person that they are. I want to shake them so hard and tell them that they are loved regardless, and that I will wait for them to realize.

If I turn that around to myself, then - suddenly it is a different matter entirely. The rules change. The whole game changes. It is no longer applicable. Every grand gesture is the bare minimum. Nothing I do is special or sacred. Are you proud of me? Not yet, but I will make sure you are. I have to be extraordinary! Don't you understand? I need to be remembered and I need to know that I mattered!

You can say it's trauma, and you're probably right. If you spend twelve years being told by your peers that you are wrong and bad and you can't understand why, you can only try to mould yourself into something more presentable and even that is wrong and bad - it grinds you down until you are dust and you are trying to scrape what is left of yourself off the floor and into some semblance of a human being again.

I apologize a lot, and I apologize for apologizing. If I say sorry enough, then people might forgive me my ultimate sin: being me. And if they forgive me, maybe I can forgive me, too.

A true monster would wrap itself up in all of this hatred and grow stronger because of it. I think that's what makes the idea of a monster such a difficult metaphor to work with. If you love a monster, it is no longer a monster. If you enjoy being haunted, are you still being haunted?

This is, undoubtedly, the great war of my life. I do not know if, when I die and my organs have been shared out, and I am finally carved up and empty, lowered into the ground to provide nourishment one last time, I do not know if I will have died liking myself. I hope I do. I hope one day I find a way to look in the mirror and not flinch. I hope every part of me becomes beloved by me. I hope that if I am a monster, I am a gentle one, that if I am haunting my own life, then I am doing it benignly.

I hope you find that same peace, if you are looking for it. Friend, I can call you friend because you have held my heart and you did not dig your thumbs in, let's sit for a while longer. I have more to tell you. I think we have time. We are not out of the forest yet, and the world is yet to end. There are more stories to tell.

5
the impossibility of you ever knowing how this felt

All of this, all of this - it's a shout into the void. I desperately want you to know that I'm out here. I am orbiting like a lonely moon and it seems like you cannot see me, and oh, I just want to be noticed. I want you to understand what it's like to be among the stars like this. I am trying so hard to tell you.

The call of the void, that call to oblivion, well, whatever that is, this is not that. This is a call from the void. Can anybody hear me? There is so much shouting, so many people trying to do exactly this - get your attention and try to make it count.

We've established so much already, I don't want to be forgotten, I want you to write something beautiful

- but what about this? I'm lonely. It's lonely out here for an autistic soul.

It's not easy to make friends. I'm not good at it. I'm more than a little afraid of people my own age, I worry they'll judge me for my lack of achievements and my lack of life milestones. They have jobs, careers, houses, families, *normal people things*. I have - well, I have enough random facts in my head to do quite well at *University Challenge*, and I might be a monster or have a monster following me, maybe both, maybe neither.

I don't know what I'm supposed to talk about when I meet people. Our points of reference are so different. 'What do I do?' I write. 'It's pretty solitary. When I write I disappear for days and I forget to sleep. Oh, the publishing industry? It's pretty complicated and I barely understand it if I'm honest. It's not worth explaining it just to complain for a few sentences. No, there's not good money in it. That's really not why I'm doing this. So, how about you, anyway, what have you been up to?'

See, it doesn't really work, does it? I'm not sure how

I'm supposed to behave. I feel like a feral animal that's being coaxed into playing with the other dogs. My mum has a Romanian rescue dog, and he's come a long way since she got him, but he still seems baffled a lot of the time by the comforts of a house. He's a very good dog, but being a pet doesn't come naturally to him.

That's kind of how I feel.

My mum's other dog, a saluki cross, is just a bit daft. She's harmless enough, but forever getting into trouble. She doesn't seem to understand what she's done wrong most of the time, and once again, I relate to her pretty hard.

I don't even particularly like dogs, which I'm pretty sure is some kind of cardinal sin, but anyway.

So, if I'm scared of people, and I don't go outside as we've established, what right do I have to complain that I'm lonely? I live with nine other people, surely that's impossible, besides? And yet, and yet. It feels unfairly possible. It's like a physical ache, sometimes. I want so desperately to have someone outside of my family who I can talk to in real life, not just over the internet. I love my internet friends dearly, but we are separated by hundreds if not thousands of miles, and time differences as well. I know them in a way I may never know someone in real life, so many late-night conversations revealing secrets that are kept secret between us, but still. But still. The ache remains for face-to-face communication.

There used to be an autism group locally, about fifteen minutes away, but it closed down. There's been nothing put in place to replace it. I have looked for creative writing courses, but again, there is just nothing out there. Whether it's a case of underfunding or lack of interest, I don't know.

I know it's not uncommon to not have friends as an adult. People drift apart and are closer to their own families, their own little packs. But it still hurts. There's still that *want* there. It doesn't go away just because you try to be rational with it.

There are only so many events you can drag your dad to because he starts to get tired of it. I feel so bad every time I do so. He will never quite grasp what I like about, say, Phoebe Bridgers. He will never know what it meant to me to see Moon Song and Sidelines performed live. For me, it was everything. For him, it was obligation. I want somebody to be there by choice, because they enjoy the same thing I do. I just - genuinely - don't know how to find this person.

This person needs to be the most patient person on earth, to boot. They need to be understanding of my anxiety, of the fact I don't drink, of the fact I don't like crowded places or dark cinemas. They have to understand that I can and will cancel plans right down to the last minute. They have to understand that I might accidentally offend them by saying the wrong thing.

I am not exactly who you'd choose as a best friend.

Maybe right now you're yelling at your book, saying you'd be a great friend. Well, I mean, you're welcome to get in touch. I know at least out of the two of us that *I'm* not a serial killer (way too much effort involved, I'd rather just have a nap).

Of course, it is the human condition to be the only one who has ever known how it feels to be you. I don't know why I find myself recurringly surprised by this. We are trapped in our own heads, and as much as I have tried to describe how I use language, I know that, ultimately, it's just me in here. I'm the only one who truly knows me, who truly knows what I mean. I don't love that as an idea, but it's the best we've got. I think that's why I find online friendships easier; it's text-based, by its very design, and whilst it lacks nuance, it makes up for this in quantity. You learn to sift through and discover the person, and you can, in time, learn to love them.

I think I'm a little bit in love with all of my online friends. Is that normal? I don't know. I think, perhaps, I'm just lucky enough to have found this amazing group of people who don't mind that I'm a little strange at times. And, in turn, they get to be a little strange at times too. It's only fair, after all.

I'm drawn to people who have strong opinions, for better or for worse, to people who can and will infodump about their favourite thing. I love receiving what are essentially hastily typed-up essays about things, it's honestly so so great. I feel so lucky to have that.

I think the thing about friendship is that it's like any other relationship, it requires a great deal of work to keep it running smoothly. Especially with online friendships, where you are battling language barriers and time differences. The distance hurts, sometimes, and my brain can't quite wrap itself around the fact that I've never actually met these people, when I feel like I know them so well. It's such a strange thing to experience, and I wonder how you're feeling now, whether you feel like you know me because you've read an abundance of my words. Have you sifted through the nonsense and discovered who I really am? Do you think you understand me? It's weird to think about, isn't it?

I wonder if there is anyone twenty years in the future reading this. Does it make sense to you at all? Is this all hideously out of date? We think about people in the past and consider them to be somehow alien to us, like they couldn't possibly understand being alive today.

Humans, though, have always been human.
Almost to a fault. I hope, dear future reader, you
can acknowledge this, and know that I was just
as human as you are, both fallible and brilliant in
equal measure, and prone to making the same dumb
mistakes and choices as anyone else.

This forest of ours, it reaches across time and space
in a way nothing else can. You can return to it as
many times as you'd like, if you want to. I'll always
be here. This has, strangely, become a home for me.
You are officially talking to a ghost. Boo.

INTERLUDE

a monster, in three parts

1/

monster says
love the shape of you curled up crying
monster says
your footfalls on the snow sound like sighing
monster says
every weekend is another week dying
monster says
don't play 'what's the time?' without an escape plan,
darlin'

monster says
you never loved me enough to put the time in
monster says
you only really cared when i helped you rhymin'
monster says

i don't photograph well enough to bring the dimes in
monster says
your catholic guilt is appropriated land and you're
lying

2/
keep
it
weak
(there is so much left to say)
keep
it
holy
(i will return to bite again)
keep
your
words
(your power is the well of all things)

3/

(the monster never loved me nobody loves me
quite like the monster i am the monster and i have
never met the monster i am sharp toothed and dull
toothed and i have claws and i have fingernails and
i have grey eyes and i have black eyes like the void
void VOID VOID VOID and the monster never loved
me nobody loves me quite like the monster this is an
endless cycle we repeat we repeat we repeat)

the only thing inside me is the void where i should be

The monster wants to get out. When I was twenty-one years old, I wanted to die so completely that I almost did. I didn't even want the inhale exhale of relief. I just wanted it to stop. Just to stop. No more sunshine, no more sleep, no more nice things. Just let it be an ending. My teeth hurt from crying so hard. I wasn't numb, I'd passed through numb and come out the other side and I was so upset, so desperately upset at the world, I couldn't stop crying.

I told my mum, I told her that she needed to do something because I was so scared of what I would do if she didn't. She asked me what I wanted her to do. I told her I didn't know. She called the doctor and got me an appointment. The doctor printed out a quickly googled page on depression and handed it to me.

I didn't die. But god, I wanted to.

I could enumerate the number of failings but there are too many to count. I could try to figure out how many times it's felt like I've been left on my own to fend for myself. It seems to be a recurring pattern, we think we have found the solution, something that will help, *someone* who will help, and then they go away. It's exhausting. It's so exhausting.

My brain tries to eat itself a lot. When I can't sleep my thoughts start to spiral and I go to the dark places. I am passively suicidal, in as much as if I were in the car and another car hit us and everyone else could be fine but I died, that would be kind of ideal. It would be sad, for a little while, but at least I wouldn't be to blame for it.

It's horrible to think about these things, to actively wish for them at times. I know it's fucked up. I know it's not normal. I know most people don't think about this sort of thing at all. I hate that my brain takes me there and that I can't crawl back out again. It's scary, not being in control.

It's difficult to cure a depression that is based on circumstance rather than brain chemistry. If you've read this far, then you can probably understand that being depressed is something I think I'm probably allowed to be without being questioned too strongly on the matter. It's worse during the winter months - god, November, December, January and February, I'm useless to you. Strangely, this year, whilst November was bad, December hasn't been so bad so far. I think it's because it feels so impossibly un-Christmassy, that I kind of think it might still be May? The blackness isn't creeping in, at any rate, though we still have most of the month to go, so we shall see.

The monster that is depression has been with me since I was a teenager, and I took antidepressants for a long time even though they make my anxiety a lot worse, if you can imagine that. There's also the withdrawal symptoms, which I refuse to go through again. The brain zaps anybody who has experienced the brain zaps, they will tell you the truth of them and how horrible they are.

There is no real opportunity to seek help for mental health in the area either - waiting lists are years long just for a consultation, and when I was in the system, psychiatrists and psychologists left so regularly that it was impossible to strike up a lasting rapport with anybody, let alone getting around to fixing anything. I was booted from the system when they told me there was nothing more they could do for me, which was a shocking statement given the lack of care I'd received at that point.

Depression is difficult to describe to somebody who has never experienced it. The black dog is such a good descriptor to somebody who can recognize it, but to somebody who has never been there, it's useless. It seems impossible to tell someone that you want to die, that you want it to be over, that you're done, finished, so fucking tired, when they just don't understand. They either overreact or underreact, there is no reaction that actually works. I think, perhaps, if you have not been in the trenches of it all, you will never understand, and god, I do envy you that.

I think I could believe in monsters if you told me that that was what caused depression. If you told me it was demons whispering to me, I'd probably buy it. It doesn't seem entirely of this earth, the way it overtakes and reshapes me. I can be fine one day, and then feel myself slipping away, knowing that something is wrong but unable to put a finger on it until it's too late. *It's just a bad day*, until it isn't. Until it's all bad days, all the time. For months at a time. It goes beyond the call of the void, the call of the void is a fucking delight compared to what's going on in my head.

And yet I am powerless. Despite wanting it all to end, it's never in an active way. It's always that passive *wanting wanting wanting* but never *doing*. I guess I'm lucky for that, like maybe I should be grateful or something. I don't feel very grateful though, to be honest.

you have to do impossible things, all the time, do you see?

I told you I want to make my parents proud. I was not lying or exaggerating. It feels, sometimes, like the most important thing in the world. And I stomp my foot against it, because it's not fair that I have this burden upon me, even if I placed it there myself. I get angry about it, why do I have to do more, and better, all the time, why do I demand this of myself when nobody else is demanding it? To what end? Why do I have to be impossible? What am I gaining from this?

Of course, I have to be impossible because I am autistic and I have to beat all the odds and more just to stand a chance. But beyond that. Beyond that particular hurdle, why do I have to keep doing this?

Why do I expect more of myself than I'd ever expect from anybody else? Why do I feel like such a let-down all the time?

My self-esteem is very low, I know that. There's not much I like about myself. Most of what I do like is external, things afforded by circumstance rather than anything I've done, like the fact that I get to be related to my sister's children. I like that about myself. But I had no part in that, it's just something that happened to me. I'm grateful for it, but I can't take the credit. Nor would I want to. It's not mine to take.

My mum laughs at every impossible thing I pull out of the hat, as though nothing could surprise her any more. I kind of want to surprise her, though. I want her to really go *wow*. I want to be impossibly impossible, to do the best thing ever. I don't know what that is, but I want to do it.

It makes my standards for myself impossibly high, all of this. If I do not succeed at something that statistically very few people succeed at, then I am a failure. In that case, it is that black and white. Every rejection tarnishes me, makes me ache inside and feel all squirmy and gross.

I constantly want to ask, *what am I doing wrong, why aren't you getting this?* It cannot possibly be my fault every single time. The odds cannot be that unfairly stacked.

I am afraid of checking my emails. I sort of hate it a lot. It has been so long since I have gotten a 'win' that I cannot open my emails without muttering, *what the fuck now.*

So if I'm not cut out for this, why do I keep doing it? If it's hurting me, why not stop?

Because I want to do this, because I want that win, because I hope that I'm good enough to do it. People say my writing is good and interesting, I just happen to write about things that are difficult to sell. I wish I could put at the end of every email *please just take a chance on me, you won't regret it, I promise.* You can't do that though, you have to be professional. Which is awful, and definitely does not allow room for emojis.

So I'm writing this and already thinking about how I'm willing to go through it all over again. Reading back every sentence and wondering if it's the best it can be. Editing as I go and trying so hard to be eloquent but approachable all at once. I know I am a better writer than I was four years ago, two years ago. But damn, I need someone else to tell me that to believe it.

I think part of autism is that sometimes we have a tendency to think in extremes of things. My extreme is my writing. I don't know what yours is, but I'm sure you can think of an opinion you hold more strongly than most people might. It's hard to argue down from an extreme. It feels so concrete, so certain, so true, that to try to deny it feels like denying a fundamental part of yourself. It, again, feels like a failure, or perhaps a betrayal. You can't just let it go, it feels like it's worth fighting for.

And sometimes that's a good thing. It keeps me writing. And writing keeps me relatively sane, if a little unhinged when I'm actually trying to get published. I don't want to tell you how many words I've written in comparison to how many hours I've slept, but it's a pretty poor ratio. I've eaten at last though, so there is that.

I went to America, did I tell you that? I went to New York and Chicago. I was there for about ten days. I'd never been on a plane before and it was turbulent the whole way there and the whole way back. See, this is the thing, isn't it? Doing extraordinary, ridiculous things. You say things like *I went to America*, and it's like, okay, I suppose you did. Sounds like something you'd do. I went to the New York Comic Con, which was just so many people crammed into an admittedly large space, and I went to see the Captain America statue in Brooklyn, because I like the idea of it being dug up in two thousand years or so and somebody believing that he truly was a forgotten war hero.

Eating on the trip was impossible, I'm pretty sure I got by on a few cookies and little more than that. I was so hungry by the time I got home, and so tired too. I had my first hot meal in ten days, and then I went to bed.

I want to tell you about before I left though, because

I can say *I went to America* all blasé like that, but actually the build-up hides the truth of it all.

I have a journal entry I wrote a few months after the trip, which is pretty revealing. I'm going to paste it in here in its entirety:

> The expectation in the back of everyone's minds was this: there was no way I was getting on that plane. Nobody was denying this. It was a spoken fact, an understanding, a Get Out Of Jail Free card. The flakiest flake in the history of the world had booked a plane ticket and had never flown before. Of course there was no way I was getting on that plane.
>
> The two-and-a-half-hour trip to London does not get any easier with familiarity, usually because what I'm doing in London is always vaguely terrifying or requires a lot more of myself than I feel able to give. This time though – well. I had places to be, and very important people to see. I had, for the first time in my life, money, not a lot, in the grand scheme of things, but enough to have made the somewhat dubious choice to go to Brooklyn, home of Bucky and Cap,

home to the beautiful people, the place dreams were born in, and the place dreams so often died in.

I had a backpack that felt like it weighed as much as I did, and a letter from my doctor giving me permission to fly with my medication. I had $200 in cash and print-outs of everything I'd need, and I was terrified.

I've been terrified a lot in my life, generalized anxiety disorder and agoraphobia cover the majority of bases, to be honest, but I'd never known a fear so utterly heart-stopping as I did when we pulled up at Liverpool Street.

And then the gods looked down, smiled, and closed the Central Line.

My uncle, who my dad and I (for I had roped my dad into a free trip to New York) were staying with, lives in Shepherd's Bush, which is not a huge issue usually, I could probably do the journey by myself, and as someone with no sense of direction and a seeming lack of object permanence when it comes to instructions, that's kind of a big deal.

But this time, we couldn't go to Shepherd's Bush, we had to go to Shepherd's Bush Market, and so did everyone else who had just gotten out of work.

I don't know if you're like me - if you plan everything in your head months in advance and get it fairly settled, as though you can pre-plan the anxiety away, but this was everything I didn't need. I was tired already, I was hungry (who eats when they're anxious? Not me!) and I wanted to get straight back on the train and go home, mostly.

I got on the tube and stood with my bag pressing against my legs, holding all its precious cargo, not knowing this journey, my eyes scudding as I tried to figure out where we were on the map above my head. My heart beat in time with the rumble of the tracks, amplifying, terrified, the certainty of bad bad BAD coming my way.

I would never get on that plane.

All too soon, the tube pulled in to the station, and like a gush of water we all streamed out, me into unfamiliar streets, my legs wobbling beneath me, my breathing coming in uncontrollable gulps, the darkness around my vision deepening, and my dad leading the way, his fast pace so much faster than I could manage, stumbling, the weight of the bag on my back, the weight in my head that was yelling at me to stop, to stop this, to do anything to stop this.

I started to lag behind, and then I stopped. I couldn't see, couldn't breathe, I was crying, and whilst 'crying in the streets of London' is probably a good name for a poem, it's a terrible thing to actually do.

Being scared is primal, animal, and it doesn't adhere to logic. It just is, and is, and is, until it's not again.

In that moment, I thought I could have died. And been relieved for it.

My dad doubled back, gathered me to him, walked me to the flat and tried to calm me. I was - a mess. I don't really remember much of those twenty minutes or so, so overwhelmed by how afraid I was, just that it was unfair - unfair that I was doing something I'd wanted to do since 2014, and I was ruining it. My brain was ruining it.

We got into the flat and my dad called my mum, and she told me – you know what, I don't remember what she told me. That it was all right, probably. That it was only money. That everything would be fine. We turned on the television and watched *Pointless* together, and the final round was stops on the Greater Anglia train line. We laughed at that – and named all the stops I'd just been through on the way to London. Every stop I'd counted down, every anxious moment. In my uncle's living room, I won with three Pointless answers, and I started to breathe again.

We had to stop talking eventually, my mum had things to do, she couldn't sit with me all night as I hiccup-cried through the phone. We had an early start tomorrow, and we had to get to Gatwick.

She told me it was okay. That I didn't have to get on the plane. But that I should. Because I had wanted to do it. How many times in my life had there been things I'd wanted to do but couldn't?

The news came on, jolting me, because it wasn't *Look East* like it should have been. I don't know why I expected it to be. The world felt alien and wrong and I was exhausted and wrung out.

I went to bed, my Kindle in my hand, reading stories about Steve and Bucky and New York.

And then the next morning, I woke up.

I wanted to include that because it's honest. It's a different kind of honest to what I write now. If you've read *How To Be Autistic*, you'll recognize the style. It seems entirely at odds when compared to how I'd tell you the story now, but it needed telling, and this is the rawest version I have of it.

Impossible things, eh?

They're kind of a lot.

wildling, made tame

Authority for authority's sake terrifies me. Anyone who seeks that level of power over another person terrifies me. Whether it's a police officer, a therapist or a teacher, I find myself actively rebelling against authority that I am supposed to respect with no reason to do so.

I understand that my experiences are not universal, and that most people have had nothing but good experiences with all of these professions. But I can't help it. I was raised to respect authority figures, and it ended up hurting me so badly that I will never make that mistake again.

I have told this story before, so I will be brief, because I do not enjoy reliving it. In high school,

there was a teacher who took it upon herself to
ensure that I never got to go home, whether I was
sick or whether it was a panic attack, whatever.
I was struggling not only with undiagnosed autism,
but also severe anxiety, and school was hell.
I desperately wanted to leave, all the time. That I
wasn't allowed to is where it all stems from – the
I want to go home. I have PTSD as a result of four
years of emotional abuse from this teacher, and she
is the one I have nightmares about. I am so angry,
because I trusted her. I thought she was on my
side. I was always told to respect teachers, and so I
respected her. I did whatever she said. She made up
lies about me and reported every perceived slight
to my mum. I collapsed in her classroom and I was
still not allowed to go home.

It upsets me even typing it out now, even knowing
she's dead. She can't hurt me any more, I know that
rationally, but my brain is still so scared of her.
I hate her for what she did to me, for how she made
me so afraid, for how she gave me a life mantra
that is based around fear. How I can't go outside
anywhere without thinking it. My life will never
be the same because she decided she was going to

torture a child, and she did it so successfully that even now I can't breathe properly as I type this.

No more of this, a chapter abandoned. Not everyone needs to be remembered. We must be careful who we immortalize. We move on now. We need to find the light again. It will be morning before long.

INTERLUDE
this is the plan

i'm going to run away
with a brand new name
and then,
i'm going to write a thousand books
like postcards trying to explain where i went to
because that's what i know how to do
(and wherever you go, there you are)
i'm going to stick a pin in a map and disappear
and in a small bookshop there, there'll be a paperback
with a new name and a new story to tell
and god, it'll be magnificent for a while
and i'll keep running because in the end i realized that's
what i needed to do to keep myself
i'm a prey animal, baby, and that sticks to a person's
bones
(wish you were here)

i'm going to curate an entire life in an apartment a
thousand miles from here
and i'm going to watch a different sunset
and i'm going to write about it
i'm going to fall off the edge of the world
and drift off into space
hold my breath 'til i freeze over
fall back to earth as dust
shooting stars, if you blink you'll miss me
i want to be careless, darling
embedded in every tome
every keystroke
goddamn, i want to be careless.

THIS WAY
AT WAY
OTHER WAY
NOT SURE
D BE
OSSIBLY
WHO KNOWS

9

wolf on fire: a novel

There is the apocalypse man, who has lived many lifetimes, and there is the boy who saves him, who has lived just one. This is the book I wish I could write. The book that maybe in twenty years I will write, when I am better and smarter and wiser. When I know how to use my words without tripping. I feel as though I write like a child, as though this is little more than crayon smudgings and I cannot yet make anything beautiful.

It's a lofty goal, isn't it, to want to create something beautiful?

I have wanted to write since I was a child. It is the only thing I have ever known how to do, and I want to do it well. It is frustrating to want to be able to do something and not to be able to do it. Like if I maybe tried a little bit harder, I'd manage it. It's almost within reach, and yet...

Writing is a translation tool. My brain uses language to communicate how I feel to myself and to others, and by writing it down, I can push these words towards you like an offering. But it's flawed, you see, because what a word means to me might not be what it means to you. In the same way we can never truly describe pain in a way that is meaningful, we cannot describe the lived experience of ourselves either. But god, we can try.

I think being neurodivergent, I rely on this translation tool more than a neurotypical person does. Words have a clarity that body language lacks. And yet, people obscure with words. People lie, they misspeak, they don't say what they mean. Sometimes, we simply don't have the words. So far, I have written fourteen thousand words trying to describe what it is like to be inside my head, and I don't know how successful I've been. What have you been imagining as you've been reading? Are we in the forest? Are we by the campfire? When I mentioned glow stars on the ceiling, did you picture them? What about the monster? What did it look like to you?

When I try to explain how trauma has changed me, how I wish I were different, how I wish things had been different, it sounds like I am wishing for time travel. There is no way to change the past. And yet, we all have things we would change, don't we? A few tweaks, here and there, some major, some small.

Some things are constants, though. My sister's children are immutable. If time travel requires that I change something that results in losing them, then I will never step on the butterfly. I will remain right here, and I will be grateful, because I get to know them and love them and watch them grow, and if they are the fish hooks in my skin that keep me here, then it was all worth it, every single second of it, because they are the brightest part of my life.

God, though, don't you just wonder, sometimes? I wonder who I could have been, what I could have been, whether I'd have the same name, the same ideals, the same morals, the same everything. Quick, what would my monster look like if I had not been hurt? Would I have a monster at all?

The truth of it, though, is that trauma, day to day, is very boring. It's the same nightmares, the same flashbacks, the same anxiety, the same fears, replayed over and over like a skipping record. And you know, deep within you, that it's boring. That it's over. That you, if *survived* is too strong a word, at least lived through it. It's over. So why does it still ache like a healing scar?

Perhaps because it is one. It's not death by a thousand cuts, but it's certainly a bloodletting. A culmination of years that results in you being a different person to who you expected to be. And you are allowed to be angry about that, all that spilt blood, all that spilt potential.

I am so angry. I don't know how to let go of that, yet. The person who hurt me is dead. Has been dead for over two years now. And yet, every couple of nights, I bring her back to life and she hurts me whilst I sleep.

I want to go home.

All my nightmares are the same. Repetition. Always with the repeating themes. I am not a creative person, perhaps trauma has stifled that. Instead, I get the same nightmares over and over. I cannot get home. Something is stopping me from getting home. I will never get home, and even if I do, home won't look like home any more.

When home burns down, where do you have left to go?

My childhood is not ashes, but it feels like it sometimes. Everything is smeared with grey and charred at the edges. It seems as though there was more bad than good, everything is more monochrome than it should be, and everything repeats in this awful way, and *I just want to go home.*

I know, objectively, that I live in a house, and it's a very nice house, and I am very lucky to have a roof over my head and a loving family to live with. I know that mourning the loss of my childhood home is not something that is logical, I know that it is a metaphor for something I cannot put into words as easily as I'd like. The home I grew up in saw some of the worst of me, and yet, perversely, I want to go back. Like, maybe I *could* change things, maybe I could overwrite the bad. Maybe if the version of me that I am now stood on the same stairs as fifteen-year-old me did, I would realize that it didn't all burn down and take me with it.

I have to make something beautiful out of all of this, because the alternative is that there is nothing here but ugliness, and I refuse to accept that. Perhaps it is churlish to throw this strop and to dig my heels in and demand beauty from such a situation, but I am going to demand it. Without romanticizing it, without making it something I loved, I still want to shape it into something I can look at and show people.

It might be the only option I have. What else is there to do? Steep in it forever, leaving it to be ugly and to eat me up until it's all I have? Let me tell you lies about Vincent Van Gogh drinking yellow paint because he wanted his insides to be beautiful. This is my yellow paint. I need my insides to be beautiful too. If they are, maybe I can be okay with what happened.

I have wanted to be in a crowd, packed in so tightly I can barely move, and to sink to my knees and just scream. And to never stop screaming, not even when my throat starts to bleed. I think about the catharsis of it, the primal animal urge of it, the way it transcends language entirely and becomes noise, urgent, desperate noise, and people have to pay attention to that, they have to pay attention to me screaming, because you can't ignore it. You just can't.

We circle back then, to wanting to be remembered. The scream is one such memorial. If I scream loudly enough, will I make a mark on you? Will it scar you the same way I was scarred? Will you go home and tell somebody about it, the way I folded to the ground and the way I ripped myself open? Is that beautiful? Is it?

We read poetry and we feel changed afterwards. Perhaps the scream is a form of poetry. Poetry transcends prose, I feel, because it is both looser and tighter all at once. I can tell you about the monster in paragraphs here, but the monster in a poem? Oh, that's a different beast entirely, free to gnaw at the true marrow of the bone.

I like poetry, even though I am bad at it. It is not something that is readily taught, and so I do not know the rules. Granted, I barely know the rules of prose either, but at least the teachers gave it a shot. With poetry, I am left adrift, and I do not understand, but god I want to try anyway.

When poetry is read aloud, I feel like I am transcending myself, the rhythm of it! It's all about the rhythm of it, the bumps in the road as the words skip across the tongue. I would call it pretty, but pretty isn't a big enough word. I feel so so lucky to live in a world where poetry exists. Humans do this, they write, they create, and I am lucky enough to experience it, and, perhaps, to know a small part of what they're feeling.

The boy who saves the apocalypse man, he understands. His superpower is empathy, you see. It does not take several lifetimes to learn to wield it, and he knows that. I think, sometimes, we forget that. The online world, particularly, lacks nuance, lacks the cadence of spoken language, and so we lose the empathy that comes with it. We are often not our best selves. We can be reactionary, we can be quick to judge. So much money depends on us engaging with people we disagree with. Our two-minute hate has been monetized. We forget how to be soft.

There are a lot of traumatized people out there, and we need to find that softness if we are all to survive. A lot of us are backed into corners, and when we are backed into corners, our monsters may bite. The stereotype of the perpetuity of the abuse cycle is a lie, it is an excuse of those who wish to hurt us or who have already hurt us to justify what they did or want to do. I want to do better than what was done to me. I want to hold out a hand and be the guide through the snowstorm. Trauma is not some magical gift that bestowed this upon me, don't get me wrong. I do not want to say that what happened to me was good or positive or that it made me stronger than I would have been otherwise. I refuse that narrative. But by living through it I am allowed to try to be better than the people who hurt me. If it is a hydra, I can go straight for the heart rather than cutting off a head and risking two more.

I want – I want to spend a lifetime writing, if you'll let me. If you'll indulge me on this. I enjoy it, even though it is terrifying. Are you judging me right now? I have to wonder, you see. Nothing exists in a vacuum, and this is no exception. Are my crayon smudgings good enough? Clear enough? I just wanted to make something beautiful, after all. I don't know if this is beautiful. It's too soon to tell. Can I write about myself, a thing I dislike, and make it beautiful? Is that what it means to create something transformative?

This thing, what I'm doing now, language, trying to get into your head and tell you stories, this haunting, the ghost by your shoulder whispering in your ear, it's all I know how to do, in the end. So I want to be good at it. I want to one day write about the apocalypse man and the boy who saves him.

In the meantime though, I have this and this and this, and this isn't nothing. Arguably, right now, it's everything, as it eats my hours and makes my wrists ache. Creating something, anything, is a time sink, is a risk/reward without odds to gamble upon. It's scary. I am telling so many truths, so many secrets, I am sending my dispatches from the end of the world and I am hoping they find you well.

It's all just words, but I hope they mean something to you. I hope the signal is strong. I hope I'm getting through.

i am in love with cities, i am terrified of fields

I was so certain I would move to London when I grew up. I, surprisingly, adore London. I love that there are so many people and that anonymity is almost guaranteed. The mixing of cultures is a gift, and to hear so many different languages just walking down a single street is like a certain kind of witchcraft. I love the underground, that it seems to take only forty-five minutes to get anywhere you want to be, and that your journey is broken up into so many little segments, it's so easy to catch a breath when time comes in nice little sections like that.

I do not live in London. I live in a village in the countryside, where, on a clear night, you can hear the train from a few towns away, or perhaps the cows from the farmer's field. The view from the kitchen window is that of crops growing tall, and then taller still, until they are taller than me. The sky is clear of light pollution, and planets and stars are easy to see. The moon is large and a frequent visitor, unobscured except for a single telegraph pole. The sunsets are a painting splash of oranges and yellows, cast wide and low over the field.

It's beautiful.

It's arguably impossibly claustrophobic.

The monster that is my anxiety is large and overbearing to the point where going out is nearly impossible most days. My life is very small, very contained, and most of the time I can get my head around that. I do not drive, could not even if I wanted to, due to the medications I take. The problem with the countryside is that it is difficult to leave on foot, even if you want to. There is simply nowhere to go. What is a sprawling piece of chocolate box perfection becomes akin to a prison, and it's as much my mind's own doing as it is the fault of poor transport links.

My family is endlessly patient with me, of course. My dad will drive me anywhere I want to go, and I often feel bad for using up both his time and his diesel. The idea of calling a taxi, of going somewhere and having to rely only on myself to get home, is so so scary to me. I wish I could do it, I know other people can do it, and yet I am scared that in the moment I would become paralysed, I would not be able to save myself. The fear of not being able to get home, even when it makes no sense, is startlingly real, and if anyone can get in the way of me, it is myself.

My brain turns inwards when I am by myself. As much as I desperately want to live independently, not being around other people causes intrusive thoughts so vile and awful that they scare me. I spiral downwards and downwards until there is nowhere left to go, until it is so very dark and I cannot see the sky. I scare myself. I become the monster again.

I am grateful, then, to live with my family, despite the noisiness and the bustle of it all. It grates, a lot, that I do not live the life I had anticipated, that London is so far away, and that I cannot blend into a crowd and go out in the evening on a whim, just because there was something on that I wanted to see. I become irrationally jealous of people who take this kind of freedom for granted, to know that there is so much on their doorsteps and they are not taking advantage of it. So many museums, so much music, so much possibility. It is almost impossible to imagine the contrast of it.

I want to be more, oh, so much more. I want to be more than the intrusive thoughts that loneliness creates, I want to have both the resources and the mental wellness to live in a place that is so fully alive. I want to look out of the window and see people. The world feels so small when the cast of characters never changes. No new faces, no new quirks to learn about.

It feels like a riddle to solve. How do I leave this place in a manner I can both afford and sustain mentally? It's a trap, you see. If I am well enough to live on my own, then the government will not support my benefits, and if I do not receive my benefits, I cannot afford to live on my own. It would be nice to live off of writing, but unless you are both very lucky and very good, it's not sustainable.

The city beckons, often, and I drag myself to it when I can. My dad will drive me, or take the train with me. Of course, the pandemic changed things, it changed everything. But for a while there, we were regular visitors, almost.

The pandemic knocked my street smarts out of me, and any confidence I had built up about the outside world. I had been agoraphobic before, and the pandemic made it easy to be inside, it was hardly an adjustment at all for me. It was hard to miss going out when going out caused so much anxiety, and so, whilst the rest of the world struggled, I found new friends online and new things to write and learn about.

Shifting back to a world that has reopened is an adjustment I haven't quite managed yet. I wish I could say I had, but the yawn of anxiety surrounds me and it's easier to cancel plans than to see them through. I don't like this, I will tell you that much.

It scares me how easily the anxiety got its claws into me and shoved them down to scrape the bone.

I have written, before, about not being in photographs. Part of this is my own doing - I hate what I look like and that only seems to have gotten worse as time goes by. I suppose the other part of it is my own doing too - the anxiety keeping me from going on the family trips out, missing out on moments that matter, those golden moments that should shine so bright in my memories. It's really fucking hard to reconcile, to see so many photographs and to be absent from all of them. I am a ghost, haunting a family from the comfort of its own room. It is strange and I do not like it. I find no comfort in it. God, how do you find comfort in being so absent from life?

There was a beautiful time, around my book being published, when life shone so bright with opportunity and I was bold, so bold, so born to do this, and I faced the world and showed my teeth and I was not afraid. I wanted to create a legacy, and I was going to do so. It was not easy, my anxiety ate at me the entire time and I needed so much

support, but god, it was worth it. I felt briefly
invincible.

It was September of 2019. The world was on the
brink of an ending. It was all about to close down
and we had no idea. I had no idea. I was beautifully
alive and I was a part of the bustle of things, and
nothing could go wrong. I had done the one thing
I had always wanted to do - to publish a book,
and people wanted to talk to me about it. It was
everything I had wanted. It was all I wanted.

So, of course the world ended.

I'm not saying the pandemic happened to spite
me, but god, it certainly feels like it sometimes.
Suddenly every open door slammed shut, and I
was on my own again, separated from the world by
something that was deadly and real and impossible
to comprehend at first. I lost a lot of weight in those
first few months, my anxiety draining it out of me
until I just stopped watching the news and counting
up the numbers.

I had to live in a kind of ignorance, as much as I

could manage to scrape together. I wrote, because
that was what I knew how to do, I queried agents
and publishers, but the world was so uncertain
that the publishing world was more cautious than
ever before, and my writing is at best niche, at
worst unmarketable. I wrote and abandoned so
many books, so many poems, another memoir, just
thousands and thousands of words left without a
home because of this weird fluke of a virus.

The world is back now, though, isn't it? So why aren't
I? Why am I struggling so much? Why can't I get
my feet under me? I was brave before, why can't I
be now?

I am thinking about screaming again.

I was never fearless, but god, I could say I was
reckless. I made plans and they happened. I left the
house. I saw more than crops and fields, heard more
than trains and cows. The loss is awful. I want it
back. I want, I want, I want.

I don't know how to fix this. I really wish I did.
This feels like the most hopeless chapter of all.

Of all the things I have bounced back from, of all the fears I have, this being left behind is the one I just can't shake. I compare the image I had of myself at fourteen with who I am now, and I wonder if I am lacking. I am not in London. I am as close to nowhere as it is possible to be. I don't like it here, I don't like being trapped inside.

I have to believe that I am not the only one who feels like this. Please, if you relate to this, know that you are not alone. I also have to believe that it will get better in time. It must do. They speak of unprecedented times, but they really were, weren't they? We weren't ready for them, we lived through them, it's fair, I think, to be shaken by it.

Part of writing this, this letter, this book, whatever it is for you, is to try to open a door. If I can sneak into the world again, if I can make a little bit of noise, perhaps I can add a few new storylines to the plot of my life. I am choosing the impossible option, the option that requires me to be briefly extraordinary. If you are reading this, somebody believed in me. Somebody opened the door for me. I promise I will make the most of the opportunity I have been given.

The thing about opportunities is that they give you an astonishing privilege to pay them forward, and so I hope that, in reading this, something resonates, some pull across the universe from me to you, that speaks to you and makes you feel less alone, that glow of comfort that can only be found from being seen.

I am brave up until the point where I am not, and my reserves are running low right now. I want a future where I am in the photographs. Where I don't cancel plans for that heady rush of relief. Where I can figure out a way to leave this village and to get myself home again.

I want to go home is embedded in the very fabric of me – it's a hard one to beat.

I have to believe it's possible though. Because the alternative is more fields, more endless horizons showcasing the same sunset. I want different sunsets, I want to see the moon in different skies. I want a thousand different windows and a thousand different views. I want to know what wanderlust feels like.

I know we have built this forest for the two of us, so I want to take the opportunity to look around, to see the sky through the trees and to feel the bark under my fingertips. It is good to be outside.

I will go outside again, I promise. It will just take a little time.

the only thing i know how to do will destroy me

I have told you that writing is the only thing I know how to do. Which lends a certain problem: in doing so, I have to let people read it. And people will judge me, over and over, will rate my life out of five stars and review it, and I have to live in a world where this happens and somehow not go insane with it all.

I do not google myself. That was one of the first things I learnt. It is scary to exist on the internet, and when I gave myself this name, I expected it to be one of many, and for it to be temporary and disposable. I did not expect to attach a life to it, to attach books and the inklings of a career to it. For it to be the recipient of awards. I do not remember where this name came from, except that I stole my surname from ol' Edgar Allan, because I wanted to imagine one of my books sitting beside his one day. I admit I did not understand book categorization, I have yet to write anything even remotely similar to his works, and I doubt I ever will, but it was a nice dream, and a little bit of motivation when I needed it most.

I liked the idea of being able to disappear if I wanted to. The beauty of the internet is that it can be as forgetful as it is permanent, and especially early on, it was very easy to stop existing. Now though, now I definitely exist.

Isn't that what I wanted? All along? Isn't that what I've been saying to you, what I've been begging for?

Well, I suppose I contain multitudes.

Yes, I want to exist and to be remembered and to change the world a little bit. I want to write books! I want people to read them, that's the point. But god, it is scary to throw your life under the microscope, especially when it all kind of happened by accident. I never expected to get published, and that is not some kind of humble brag, it is just the truth.

Publishing happened to me, I did not happen to publishing.

And yet, I want to keep doing this. I want to keep telling you stories. I wouldn't be writing this now if I didn't. I suppose I am stubborn. I don't want to give up. It's funny, I'll tell you that I'll give up the second anything gets hard, but I don't think that's strictly true. It's more self-deprecating to say, certainly, but the truth is, when I really want something, I lock my jaws down on it tight and refuse to let go.

(Unless, of course, the anxiety.)

As I get older, this urge becomes only more apparent. I need to leave a mark, a legacy, I need to leave something behind that proves that this was all worth it. All of this, the good and the bad, I need to have been here. I need you to see me. I need this to matter.

I know that one day there will be nothing left. I know that ultimately any attempt at immortality through creativity is futile. The world will continue to turn long after humans have ceased to exist. And

on a long enough timeline, even the sun will go out.
So it has to be pointless, right?

No.

I refuse to believe that any creative endeavour is
pointless just because one day there will be nobody
left to see it. Certainly, I keep doing this because
what matters is the now of it all. Your now or mine,
I don't mind, you can pick. I am talking to you
now. You are reading this now. We're back to the
old temporal problem again, you see. But isn't it
clever, isn't it death defying, to conquer time in this
manner? Isn't it a little bit magnificent? Humans, as
far as I know, are the only creatures who can do this.
It's a little like taxidermy, don't you think? We're
cheating death by preserving a part of ourselves
that both is and isn't us. It's a little bit sneaky, a
little bit dangerous.

In the act of creating, we're a little like tiny gods.

I like that, I like the *poiesis*, the creating something
from nothing. It is beautiful, it is fragile, and in the
entirety of the universe's existence, it is fucking

rare. So yes, I am driven to document what I can, even though I am so terrified of people's opinions and what they might think of me. God, I spent my entire school career being subjected to people's opinions and what they thought of me, and I didn't even sign up for that. At least this time, it's my narrative.

I love that I can do this. It's my favourite thing about me. Am I good at it? Not particularly. Will I get better at it? Hopefully, in time. Writing is the kind of thing you do get better at, the more you do it. And I do it a lot. It's kind of a thing.

Writing has somehow the most monsters and the fewest. Certainly it's the hardest thing I have to do. Right now I'm running on no sleep and my stomach is gurgling because I desperately need to eat, and my wrists are still aching from typing so much. But god, looking at the word count go up, reading the words back and not hating them, being hit with the next sentence and the one after that. Wanting to tell you this story, haunting you, coming up with metaphors and new ways to tell you things I've never shared with anyone before! It's worthy of the exclamation mark. It's such a special way to while away the hours, not just for me, but hopefully for you as well. How long have you been reading for? Are you comfortable? Do you have a hot drink, or did you have a hot drink that has now gone cold? Are you wondering about a story you might write? Do you want me to pass you the pocket knife so that you can carve your initials into the tree and watch them grow up and up towards the sky? We are so lucky! So so lucky, to be born with the ability to create. Art is a gift, truly, and we have all been given it. I don't believe there is anybody out there who can create truly bad art, not if their heart is in it. If it means something to you, then it can never be terrible. There is always something redeeming. Honestly, I believe this.

I think writing is about asking questions. Of yourself, of the person reading what you've written. I'm writing this because I fear the end of the world, and I want to understand what that means. Which end of the world it is that I fear. Annihilation is a beautiful word for a terrible thing.

I have to believe that this is not all in vain. I have

to believe that this matters. Not just because I need it to, but because I want it to. I need it in a visceral, stomach clenching way, but I want it because it's too important not to matter. We have the opportunity to tell our stories, we can run from the monsters or we can welcome them as a part of the story, and I am doing both, right now.

I truly don't know how to do anything else. I don't know if I'd ever want to.

When I say this will destroy me, it is not necessarily a negative thing. It just means that one day, after my world has ended, my words will be the only things left of me, and they will replace me and speak for me, and my power will transfer to them, so god, I better write as much as I can and I better make it good. If we die when the last person says our name, then I suppose I ought to make it count, then. I have a finite number of hours to get all of this down in, and I want to get as much down as possible. I get destroyed either way. I want to leave something behind that will outlive flesh and bone.

Taxidermy, you see?

Or perhaps a skeleton on display in a science lab, scrubbed clean and maybe missing a couple of toes.

That's okay, I could live with that as a metaphor for what I'm doing here.

I suppose I write because I'm afraid not to. Is that it? What do you think? Is this motivated by fear or by something else? I honestly couldn't tell you. Isn't any act of seeking to be remembered at least partially motivated by the fear of being forgotten? Is there shame in that? Really? Is there anyone out there who truly wants to be forgotten? Am I just the only one being honest about it right now?

So I'll be honest. I fear being forgotten. I'm okay with that. It's true, after all. I want to be remembered. I want to have existed. This world, with enough time, it swallows people up. Is it really so silly to not want to be eaten whole?

Maybe your motivations are different. I don't know if I envy you for that or not. I kind of like being a part of this race against time, I like seeing the possibility for what I can achieve. There's a certain endurance element to writing, you know, in a very real sense it is hard to do, and harder to do well.

I want to tell stories.

It's not much, but it's all I have to offer. Other people can be doctors and lawyers and teachers and zookeepers, I don't know. For me, it's always going to be writing. It always has been.

It's worth every monster, it's worth every rejection. Yes, it hurts like hell every single time, and I will complain to the ends of the earth about the unfairness of it all, but that doesn't mean I'm going to stop. I'm stubborn, stubborn, stubborn. I want to be remembered.

So I shall be. Maybe not with this. Maybe with something else. But god, it's worth a shot, right?

INTERLUDE
if i name you it still won't be enough

you are shaped like somebody only a martyr could love,
tender lipped and you duck your head under the heat
of my gaze, monster
you are a car crash in late october, early evening skies
and your breath hanging in the air -
like smoke,
and isn't it beautiful to press the softness of your body
to the mattress and open your mouth,
wide like a prayer, if you're good then maybe it'll even
come true
heart in throat and cutting off oxygen, you asphyxiate
on all the words you couldn't swallow quickly enough
my hand on your chest,
feel the rhythm of a cascading disaster
and you know the monsters only exist at night -
so surrender 'til morning collapsing lax to the sheets

and my fingers hold the bones of your wrist like egg
shells, delicate
do you know how to be anything other than
sanctuary?
i burn to the ground in the blaze of your hollow point
pleas,
if you find me bruised, do i bruise?
and no, i don't believe in anything really –
but your eyes are black and rimmed with the same
colour the ocean boasts,
and you are mere inches away from where i need to be
so i gather, i gather you, i kiss your eyelids closed
one second past doomsday and the blood pinks your
cheeks
i apologize in gasps in gaps in the in betweens of a
good goodbye
and like snow, you fall.

i am so scared that you do not understand

We are going in circles. We are the skipping record. It has been thousands and thousands of words and I still feel the same desperation I did on the same page. The world has apparently still not ended, and yet, here we are. We are still in the forest. It is nearly morning, nearly time to leave. We are still continuing our one-sided discussion of all things. I hope I am not boring you. I hope something I have said has been valuable to you.

It is important that something has been valuable, if not everything. I hope you want to write something, or create something, or maybe just go into a crowd and scream. I hope you have gained something useful from all of this, because then this has not been a failure. I hope you understand that much.

All of this has been a missive to you as an attempt to tell you my story, as an attempt to be remembered, and as an attempt to get you to tell your own story in turn.

We are a minority whose culture has been erased from history. We cannot diagnose the dead. All we have is who we are now, so we must create if we want to see ourselves represented as who we are, and not who the neurotypicals want to fearmonger us as. If we must be the monsters they hunt, at least let's give them a damn good reason for it.

We cannot change the past. I have learnt that much, but we *can* change the future. Every time somebody speaks up, the world changes for the better. I hope you understand that I want you to be loud, that I want you to be magnificent. Because you are. You are magnificent. You are one of my brilliant, brilliant friends who just doesn't see it yet. I want you to see it. I want you to shine.

I want to shine too. See, I'm selfish that way. I don't want attention, as such, but I do want to present this to my mum and say *look what I did*. Look what

I made. Look what the years of teaching me to love reading created. I want to tell her thank you, that she never failed me, even though I know she feels like she did. You didn't. I promise. When I was on my own, you were there beside me. You were so present that when I say *on my own* I mean that you are right there with me, because I have never truly been alone, not since the day I was born, because I always had you. None of this was your fault. I promise you, I promise you, I promise you.

I am sure there were sections that didn't make sense, that you really did misunderstand. I urge you not to take umbrage with them, or to think that I was speaking unkindly. That was never my intention. I tell stories, and this is the story I wanted to tell. It's only short, and you're close to the end now. Not much further to go.

13

i was here

Was I here? I think I was. Briefly, magnificently.
I was here. And so were you. That has to count for
something, right? Maybe it counts for everything.

There are eight billion people on this planet of ours.
That's a number beyond comprehension, don't even
try to imagine it. Eight billion people with eight
billion different stories to tell. Okay, so I don't want
the competition, but god, what a world.

In the introduction, I talked about the shadows
left blasted onto walls and pavements, and then I
talked about graffiti, and chalk on pavements. Two
very different sets of things, and yet not so different
at all. Both are reminders that someone existed.
One in annihilation, one in creativity. I think,

perhaps, that is a choice we all have to make, in the end, if we want to be remembered, if we want to create something beautiful and lasting. How will we decide to impact the world? Will we be a bomb blast or something colourful and more temporary than all of that destruction? It seems nowadays so many people choose destruction to gain attention, because it's easier to loudly hate things than it is to quietly love them. It is certainly easier to destroy than to make. These are your options, which one are you going to choose?

I choose, always, to create. It would be so easy to become a liar and a shill and a grifter, and to sell my soul to the highest bidder. I see it every day. But I don't want that, god, I don't want that.

If being honest, if telling the truth and these stories, if guiding you through the forest and back towards the edge of town, is what I have to do, if it is the course of least damage, let me choose that instead. If it is kinder, and softer, a kind of gentle nudge rather than a punch to the gut.

The end of the world haunts me, the end of my

world haunts me. And yet, I have to have hope. That this will last, somehow. That humans will carry on telling stories and making art. That the bad guys won't win. That somehow, against all odds, the world won't end.

There are eight billion ways this story could be told. This is my way. I hid what I could, but I never deceived, never lied. I wanted to tell you about the monsters, about the hauntings, about all of it. I didn't mean to scare you, and I'm sorry if I did. That was so far from my intention.

I wanted to tell you to be brave. Even when you feel like you can't be. Possibly especially then. And I know it's fucking hard to be brave. I know, I know. But I want to hear your story. The world needs it. More stories, more campfires.

We are nearing the end of our time together, for now. The forest has been kind to us, has kept us safe and dry. It has been a refuge as we have fought through the darkness together, as I have told you about all the bad days that seem to merge into one, all the ways I wish I were better or stronger or bolder.

I am a work in progress. I think we all are. I am
writing this as a work in progress. I want to come
back in a few years and tell you that things are
brighter, better. I want to show you what I can do in
another four years, another ten. I don't want this to
be the end of the story, not yet. If *How To Be Autistic*
was the violent beginning, let this be a softer middle,
still brutal in its way, but on the way to kindness.
I think I would like that.

If I am a monster, I hope you don't hate me for it. It
is, at the time of writing, the best descriptor I can
use to describe how I feel. I don't think all monsters
are bad, or wrong, I think a lot of them are just
misunderstood. And I feel that a lot, misunderstood.
I think I told you that.

It feels a little like emerging from a fever dream,
and maybe none of this happened after all. If you
wake up and I'm gone, will you remember me? Will
you let me haunt you a little while longer after the
last page?

I don't know if I found the answers I was looking for.
I know I asked a lot of questions. I think that might

be just as important, you know. Because asking questions is the first step towards finding answers, and if you find the right questions to ask, well, you're already halfway there.

I hope you asked some questions too, along the way. I'm sorry I didn't hear them. There are limitations to this format, to be sure. I hope you found some answers too, and some reassurances, and some solidarity. Maybe a little bit of comfort too, in amidst it all.

My wrists ache! It's been a long time writing. The snow warning has come and gone by now. In its place, nothing but clear skies. The forest is giving way to grass now, and as we sweep away the last of the foliage, the sun is rising.

Thank you for spending this night with me, for being my companion. I hope it was not a waste of your time. Please remember, you are alive, so alive, and you are so loved. Whatever you do, I am so proud of you. Tell your stories, sing your songs, make your art. The world needs it, now more than ever. Keep the darkness and the monsters at bay, unless you

make a friend of one of them. It's okay if you do.
A monster can be many things, and not all of them
are bad.

Good morning, good morning, look how purple the
sky is!

What a wonderful time to be alive. Despite it all,
what a wonderful time to be alive.

EPILOGUE

how to stand in a room, a beginning

Tick, tick, boom. Time's up. The Doomsday Clock ran out.

The thing is, it took a long time. And a rejection. And this book. Not in that order. I don't recall the order. But time, ultimately. It's very easy for other people to tell you that you're good enough. It's a lot harder to believe it of yourself. Come on, it's impossible, right? The monster won't let you believe it. You can pretend. You can call it impostor syndrome. But the uncomfortable squirm of your guts will call you a liar when you say that you belong.

Right up until you believe it.

It's fucking arbitrary.

I spent thirty-three years believing I didn't deserve
to do this. That I didn't deserve to tell you stories.
I spent this entire book believing that I wasn't good
enough. I swear that's the truth. As much bravado
as I had, it wasn't real. It is now. I am not the worst
writer in the world, and even if I was, I would still
be worthy of a seat at the table. Because we all have
room to grow. Writing is an innate ability, certainly,
but it is something we can strengthen. It only gets
better the more we do it, as with all art. So all that
shouting into the void, all the screaming, it was
worth something. It made me better, it made me
louder. And gradually, I began to believe that I was
worthy of what I was saying.

It was almost overnight. Like falling asleep, the
doubt was here, then gone. A publisher picked up a
novel I loved. I'd worked so hard on it. I was so proud
of it, it held all of my demons and my fears and
pieced me back together again. I spent December
with the flu working hard editing it and making it
the most perfect it could be. I sent it off, finished,
mid-January, and the editor loved it just as much as
I did. I was sure we were done, my novel, beautiful
and beloved.

And then the strangest thing happened. It was torn apart. Apparently previously unread by the head of the publishing house, it 'fell apart in the second half' and needed to be completely rewritten. Amongst other issues. I was given a year to 'fix it'. I read the edit letter. I couldn't see the problems. I felt uncomfortable. The confidence I'd gained was dissipating but not vanishing entirely. In its place was a stubbornness. I wanted to fight for this. Even if it meant walking away. I knew a younger version of me would have folded, would have taken that year and would have rewritten the novel to be whatever someone wanted it to be, for the chance to be published. So desperate to be loved, to be perfect. To be wanted. It's apparent in these pages, isn't it? I see it, too.

I walked away. I took my anxiety medication and I walked away. The novel had been good enough to win a seat at the table in the first place, so obviously I was worth something. One man's opinion didn't change that. And besides, the migraine medication I was on was setting my brain alight. I was writing poetry and creative nonfiction like never before. And I was sending it off. And it was being accepted.

The monster didn't know what to do with itself. So I turned to the monster and said 'Do you want to be in my poems?' and it said 'Yes, please'. So I wrote poetry about it.

For my next trick, maybe I'll try to convince the lovely people here to release that book of poetry. It's a messy, messy little piece of queer monster weirdness, written at three a.m. in my notes app on no sleep, but god do I love it. And god am I proud of it.

I trawled websites looking for new things to send off. I entered competitions. I won them. I was, apparently, good at this. Suddenly external validation felt less vital. Yes, still vital, but less so than before. The buzz under my skin from the monster that fed upon it was lessened, and in its place was the urge to create. I knew I could do this. I wanted to do this. I wanted to see what I could do with all this time I had to play with. I wanted to see what I could surprise myself with next.

I had so much to teach myself. Fifty-word stories, interactive poetry, two-sentence stories, all of it, I wanted to try it all. So I did. And again and again

I was invited to the table. And sure, there were rejections. But fine, I found myself screenshotting them and sending them to my friends, the monsters made small by laughing at their weird languages. Somebody told me poetry should be without emotion. I wondered what their poetry must look like.

If this book has left you feeling desperate, as though external validation is the only way to find meaning, that you will never feel love for your work yourself, then that is because that is how I felt. And then a switch flipped, and I don't know if that was getting older, getting rejected, or just something in the water, but the monster's jaws unclenched and I could finally see that it was okay. I could take a breath. I was good. I was worthy. Just as I was. The effort I was putting in was enough. I was working hard enough. My words were pretty enough. I just needed to love what I was doing. That was the missing piece. I expected everyone else to love it for me.

Rejections still hurt. Sometimes I think I have a win when really it's a loss. You never can tell in this game. But there will always be more wins coming along. It's a numbers game, ultimately. You can shotgun this to hell and back, if you want to. Or you can pick carefully. Whatever you want to do. But if you don't love it? It's all pointless.

Be your first cheerleader, your first reader, your first fan. Be your first pat on the back. I know telling you this is pointless until that switch gets flicked for you, but I need to tell you that it will happen. I don't know when or how, but it will. And when it does, god. Suddenly it all becomes fun. It's a game, suddenly. And you understand how your ancestors tamed wolves, because the monster wants to play too.

I don't write like a dying man any more. I don't write like I'm scared. I don't write like I have something to prove. I write to show off. I write because I want to be silly. I write because I want to be weird. I write because I want to do something nobody's ever done before. I write because I see a prompt and want to turn it on its head.

It's fun. As it should be.

I hope it can be for you, too.

This is the end, now. The end of a dream, of a nightmare. The sun is up. The monsters are gone. It's just you, and me, and I'm fading fast.

Goodbye. Write fast, write well, be brave.

VOID VOID VOID VOID VOID VOID VOID VOID VOID VOID
VOID VOID VOID VOID VOID VOID VOID VOID VOID VOID
VOID VOID VOID VOID VOID VOID VOID VOID VOID VOID
VOID VOID VOID VOID VOID VOID VOID VOID VOID VOID
VOID VOID VOID VOID VOID VOID VOID VOID VOID VOID
VOID VOID VOID VOID VOID VOID VOID VOID VOID VOID
VOID VOID VOID VOID VOID VOID VOID VOID VOID VOID
VOID VOID VOID VOID VOID VOID VOID VOID VOID VOID
VOID VOID VOID VOID VOID VOID VOID VOID VOID VOID
VOID VOID VOID VOID VOID VOID VOID VOID VOID VOID
VOID VOID VOID VOID VOID VOID VOID VOID VOID VOID
VOID VOID VOID VOID VOID VOID VOID VOID VOID VOID
VOID VOID VOID VOID VOID VOID VOID VOID VOID VOID
VOID VOID VOID VOID VOID VOID VOID VOID VOID VOID
VOID VOID VOID VOID VOID VOID VOID VOID VOID VOID
VOID VOID VOID VOID VOID VOID VOID VOID VOID VOID
VOID VOID VOID VOID VOID VOID VOID VOID VOID VOID
VOID VOID VOID VOID VOID VOID VOID VOID VOID VOID
VOID VOID VOID VOID VOID VOID VOID VOID VOID VOID
VOID *the single spark of light that starts this all over again* **VOID**
VOID VOID VOID VOID VOID VOID VOID VOID VOID VOID
VOID VOID VOID VOID VOID VOID VOID VOID VOID VOID
VOID VOID VOID VOID VOID VOID VOID VOID VOID VOID
VOID VOID VOID VOID VOID VOID VOID VOID VOID VOID
VOID VOID VOID VOID VOID VOID VOID VOID VOID VOID
VOID VOID VOID VOID VOID VOID VOID VOID VOID VOID
VOID VOID VOID VOID VOID VOID VOID VOID VOID VOID
VOID VOID VOID VOID VOID VOID VOID VOID VOID VOID
VOID VOID VOID VOID VOID VOID VOID VOID VOID VOID
VOID VOID VOID VOID VOID VOID VOID VOID VOID VOID
VOID VOID VOID VOID VOID VOID VOID VOID VOID VOID
VOID VOID VOID VOID VOID VOID VOID VOID VOID VOID
VOID VOID VOID VOID VOID VOID VOID VOID VOID VOID
VOID VOID VOID VOID VOID VOID VOID VOID VOID VOID
VOID VOID VOID VOID VOID VOID VOID VOID VOID VOID
VOID VOID VOID VOID VOID VOID VOID VOID VOID VOID
VOID VOID VOID VOID VOID VOID VOID VOID VOID VOID
VOID VOID VOID VOID VOID VOID VOID VOID VOID VOID
VOID VOID VOID VOID VOID VOID VOID VOID VOID VOID
VOID VOID VOID VOID VOID VOID VOID VOID VOID VOID

acknowledgements

Firstly, I'd like to acknowledge Penny, who was a very good dog.

My Tobin-y Bobin-y, who cheered me on the loudest and who I'm pretty sure is either an ancient spirit or a transmogrified frog, causing mischief and spreading so much joy, who I love to bother about everything from German pronouns to autistic werewolves. I'm so glad I get to know you.

Jay, who has had my back every step of the way, and who inspires me to be the best version of myself and to stand up for the things I believe in. Your rambles and infodumps are the best part of my day.

Grace and Arden, twin lighthouses in the dark, so

many thousands of miles away from me, giving me hope for the future.

Dio, dingus.

Mum, my first reader and the person I trust the most with my writing, and with my - everything, really. You listen to me go on for hours about my latest special interests, and you have this faith in me that I can never understand. I will keep trying to make you proud forever, no matter what you say.

Ethan, Ella, Roan, Remi and Aidan - my world revolves around you. You are the most beautiful people in my life, and I love you all to the moon and back.

I would also like to acknowledge the following people, in no particular order, for various degrees of sanity-keeping and inspiration purposes:

Dad, Joey, Rosie, Mikey, Julz, the good people at JKP who believed in this weird little book, everyone who read *How To Be Autistic* and allowed me the chance to do this again, my leaf insects for their funky little ways, the music of Julien Baker, Savannah Brown, anyone and everyone who has been patient with me when I didn't deserve it, my year eight English teacher for showing me oblivion for the first time when he told the class about the Doomsday Clock.

You, dear reader, for being kind enough to hold this in your hands and to have read to the end. I can never be grateful enough to you all. You make this terrifying scream into the void echo back and it sounds a lot like reassurance and comfort.

And to all the monsters that stalk the shadows, I owe your nips and bites and gentle howling everything in the making of me.